THE
Buena Salud™
GUIDE TO
OVERCOMING
DEPRESSION
AND ENJOYING LIFE

Newmarket Books by Jane L. Delgado, Ph.D., M.S.

*The Buena Salud™ Guide to Overcoming Depression
and Enjoying Life*

The Buena Salud™ Guide for a Healthy Heart

The Buena Salud™ Guide to Diabetes and Your Life

The Latina Guide to Health: Consejos and Caring Answers

[all available in English and Spanish]

THE *Buena Salud*™ GUIDE TO OVERCOMING DEPRESSION AND ENJOYING LIFE

JANE L. DELGADO, PH.D., M.S.

Foreword by Rosalynn Carter, Former First Lady and
Founder, Carter Center Mental Health Program

NEWMARKET PRESS

This book is published in the United States of America.

First Edition

ISBN: 978-1-55704-972-8 (English-language paperback)
1 2 3 4 5 6 7 8 9 10

ISBN: 978-1-55704-974-2 (Spanish-language paperback)
1 2 3 4 5 6 7 8 9 10

Library of Congress Cataloging-in-Publication Data .
Delgado, Jane L.
 The buena salud guide to overcoming depression and enjoying life / Jane L. Delgado ; foreword by Rosalynn Carter. -- 1st ed.
    p. cm.
Includes bibliographical references and index.
 Summary: "The book addresses: how to overcome cultural barriers to recognizing and seeking help for depression, including machismo and aguantando (enduring)   the relationship between depression and chronic conditions such as diabetes, heart disease, and arthritis   medication, therapy options, genetics, alternative treatments, and the influence of environmental factors real-life stories and the social and physical differences in how men and women deal with depression. With a ten-point program for good health and emotional well-being, this valuable guide also includes a resource section with tools to help readers take control, key questions to ask a health care provider, and advice on choosing a psychotherapist"-- Provided by publisher.
  ISBN 978-1-55704-972-8 (pbk.)
 1. Depression, Mental--Popular works. 2. Hispanic Americans--Mental health--Popular works. I. Title.
  RC537.D397 2011
  616.85'27--dc23
                              2011030733

QUANTITY PURCHASES
Companies, professional groups, clubs, and other organizations may qualify
for special terms when ordering quantities of this title. For information e-mail sales@newmarket-press. com or write to Special Sales Department, Newmarket Press, 18 East 48th Street, New York, NY 10017; call (212) 832-3575 ext. 19 or 1-800-669-3903; FAX (212) 832-3629.

Web site: www. newmarketpress. com

Design by Keira McGuinness

Manufactured in the United States of America.

This book is designed to provide accurate and authoritative information in regard to the subject matter covered. It is not intended as a substitute for medical advice from a qualified physician. The reader should consult his or her medical, health, or other competent professional before adopting any of the suggestions in this book or drawing inferences from it.

The author and the publisher specifically disclaim all responsibility for any liability, loss, or risk, personal or otherwise, that is incurred as a consequence, directly or indirectly, of the use and application of any of the contents of this book.

⌒Contents

The *Buena Salud*™ Series

T he mission of the National Alliance for Hispanic Health (the Alliance) is to improve the health of Hispanic communities and work with others to secure health for all. This has been a major challenge because although 1 out of every 6 people in the United States is Hispanic, too often health research, analysis, and recommendations do not address Hispanic lives. As information emerges about Hispanic health, it is clear that to achieve the best health outcomes for all, we need a different approach to health care in our communities. Besides providing the best health information, we need to create a new way to think about health that blends the strengths of the Hispanic community with the latest medical and technological advances.

The *Buena Salud*™ series is designed to make that happen. Each book identifies the key factors that define a health concern, the changes that each of us needs to consider making for ourselves and our family, the most up-to-date information to live healthier lives, and the tools that we need to make that possible.

The challenge is to sort through the daily onslaught of health-related information and recognize that many of the changes we need to make to improve our health we cannot do alone. Our sense of family and responsibility to our family is one of the great strengths in our community, and it is key to improving the health system. Nevertheless, to do so we all need to work together. Whether it is an uncle, a brother, a sister, or a *comadre*, we have to help each other become as healthy as possible. This series is for you because there is so much that you can do to improve your own health and the health of others.

We are at a critical moment when we can make all of our lives better. The promise of science is before us, and we must use every bit of information to care for our body, mind, and spirit. Through the *Buena Salud*™ series, we want to be your partner in making it happen.

⌒ Foreword

For the past 40 years I have worked to reach all communities with the message that mental health and mental wellness need our nation's attention and that mental illnesses can be treated and managed. In her book, *The Buena Salud™ Guide to Overcoming Depression and Enjoying Life*, Dr. Jane Delgado inspires us with the stories of men and women who have experienced depression, provides advice we can use for treating and managing it, and challenges all of us to end the stigma associated with this serious disorder.

It frustrates—and motivates—me to know that the major stumbling block to treatment is still stigma, something other advocates and I have worked for decades to overcome. Too often stigma comes from distortions about depression and other mental illnesses that we see in the media. We need voices of compassion like Dr. Delgado's that provide accurate, practical information such as that contained in this valuable guide.

I have heard from people across the country about all they have done to recover from their depression. But, sadly, many initially were reluctant to seek help. Some did not know that help was available, and others felt uncomfortable seeking help, even when it was accessible. If you or a loved one is depressed, please get the help you need. The *Su Familia* National Hispanic Family Health Helpline at 1-866-SU-FAMILIA (1-866-783-2645), available in Spanish and English, is just one of the many wonderful and trusted resources that Dr. Delgado recommends for identifying free or low-cost mental health services where you live.

Drawing from her experience as a clinician and health advocate, Dr. Delgado provides a concise guide to what you need to know about depression in its many forms, and answers the most common questions Hispanics ask about depression. She gives the reader the best online sources for information; a guide for talking to your health care provider; and tools for tracking mood, sleep, medication, and physical activity to help treat and manage depression.

I am proud to have worked in partnership with Dr. Delgado, one of this nation's most trusted health leaders, since my time as First Lady and then as part of the Carter Center Mental Health Program. I applaud her work in *The Buena Salud™ Guide to Overcoming Depression and Enjoying Life* and am confident that readers will find hope and a path for recovery and wellness.

—ROSALYNN CARTER, FORMER FIRST LADY AND
FOUNDER, CARTER CENTER MENTAL HEALTH PROGRAM

◠ Introduction

> Sara was active in so many sports that it was hard to
> keep track of all her activities. Her voice was always full
> of laughter and I could remember her playfulness. But
> as I looked at her now I knew that she had just been an
> expert at hiding her pain. She had eliminated the pain
> by hanging herself in her room. All that was left was
> her body in a coffin, surrounded by those who loved
> her and did not know the depth of her depression.

Writing about depression is very difficult because it encompasses experiences that are often devastating. Others are very intimate. Whether it was my experience with a friend, a family member, or a patient, the feelings that surround depression are usually raw and the wounds are very deep. These feelings make it essential to discuss depression; and at the same time, they make it a very difficult topic to address.

When people share the details of their experience with depression, it usually exposes their vulnerabilities and the secrets they may have buried. It takes a lot of work to do this and perhaps that is why so much effort is spent trying to make believe that depression is not real. The hope is that, like a bad dream, you will wake up and it will be gone. But that is not what happens.

Depression has at its core thoughts and feelings that make a person feel bad and refrain from doing the kinds of activities that he or she enjoys. While we are all familiar with having not-so-good feelings, too many of us tend to believe that in every instance a person should be able to make those feelings go away. And while this may be true in some cases, there may be times in your life when you may need different types of additional help to regain your ability to enjoy life.

To get beyond depression we need to understand as much as possible about it. In our everyday language, we use *depression* to cover a broad range of experiences, from the disappointments that are part of most of our lives to those times when a person is completely unable to function.

There is no single known cause of depression. Certain events may trigger depression in some people, but not in others. One person may suffer a major loss and be sad for a time, while another person experiencing the same kind of loss will have a major depressive episode. At this point there is no gene test or brain scan that can tell us definitively that someone will become profoundly depressed. Depression occurs in some people and not in others, and overcoming it requires understanding, knowledge, and concrete action.

Depression is neither a way of life nor something that just has to be endured. There is much that can be done to get to a better place. Far too many people have endured depression rather than moving away from it. None of us should spend our lives suffering, and that is why this book is so important. Life can get much better if we seek treatment for depression.

If we know that depression is common and that there is treatment for it, why are people reluctant to seek help? Several factors keep us from seeking help, including (1) our discomfort in talking about our thoughts and feelings—sometimes even our inability to do so—(2) our misconceptions about treatment, and (3) our need for tools and resources.

This book addresses these three areas in very concrete ways. Part One offers an extensive discussion of the range of experiences that characterize depression and what makes it more than simply feeling sad. The evidence presented here helps us accept that, while the values we have about work, endurance, and family sustain us, they can also be taken to an extreme and become harmful. The biology of depression is detailed in a way that helps us understand the role of genes, brain chemistry and structure, and the environment in bringing on this condition. It is also made clear that there is a relationship between depression and diseases such as diabetes and heart disease. The challenge is to understand how to value the treatment for depression as much as we value treating diabetes or heart disease. Given what we know about a happy and healthy life, a 10-Point Program for Health and Wellness is presented as a reasonable way to make the changes and adjustments that are necessary to overcome depression and enjoy your life.

Part Two focuses on putting the latest science at your fingertips when it comes to the different treatments available. You'll find a lot of information about treatment options in the media (that is, in newspapers and magazines, and on radio, TV, the Internet, and social media), but much of it is designed to be alarming, rather than informative. This section provides the facts on some of the most cutting-edge topics with respect to the treatment of depression (including light therapy) while giving the latest findings about areas where we still have many unanswered questions (such as brain stimulation therapy). It also describes the training of the different types of mental health professionals.

The final section (Part Three) gives you an array of valuable tools and resources. This section includes questions to ask your health care provider about depression, suggestions on how to pick a psychotherapist, and even a format to help you track your thoughts and feelings.

But what makes this book special is that when you read the stories, many will resonate with your life and will help you to see that you *can* have a happier life. The information in this book is intended to make life better for all—those with depression, those we love who have depression, and those of us who have to address the consequences of untreated depression. Once you recognize that there are treatment options for alleviating depression, you can take the steps you need to take. Remember that if you apply the lessons learned by others and shared in this book, as well as the findings from science that are presented here, you will be able to overcome depression and enjoy your life.

Part One

DEPRESSION HAS MANY FACES

Tomás was very intense at work because he knew it was the only way he could get anything done. He knew he had to hide what he felt because no one wanted to hear him complain. But the truth was that he couldn't enjoy the things he used to enjoy and could not find anything new that brought him pleasure. He also realized that he was very sad.

It seemed that the sadder Lourdes became, the less likely it was that anyone would speak to her. As she walked home from work, she was taken aback as she caught a glimpse of her face in a storefront. Lourdes saw that the expression on her face was one of anger. At that moment she realized that when she was sad she looked angry.

Depression has many faces. And not all those faces are the ones we expect. Any face can be the face of someone with depression. Depression can be found in the face of the child who lost a parent, the young woman who does not see a future for herself, or the older man who is tired of living. It can occur in someone who is young or old, married or single, male or female, a recent immigrant or a 10th-generation American, successful or not.

Depression touches many lives, from those who seem to have everything to those who have nothing, while at the same time sometimes skipping people who seem to be inundated with life stressors. There is no single image that encompasses all the faces of depression. While looking sad may suggest that someone is having a problem, that is not always a sign of depression. It is easy to misinterpret the expression on someone's face because how people show their emotions varies greatly from one person to another. Additionally, our ability to read facial expressions is not as good as we think, and it is often determined by our own culture and experiences.

Yvette had put up with Oscar's screaming and yelling and demanding behavior for years, but one day she had had enough and decided to it was time to file for divorce. When she told Oscar what she had done, he became very quiet and began to sob. Yvette felt terrible and it made her feel guilty that she had initiated divorce proceedings. What she didn't know was that Oscar was crying because he was upset that she had filed first and, as a result, would end up with the upper hand when they went to court.

When someone cries, we often see it as an expression of sadness or empathy. At the very least, crying is a sign of deep emotion, but, depending on the person and the situation, it may have a different meaning than what you think. A person may by crying from joy, out of frustration, out of deep feelings of regret, or maybe just to get a desired reaction from those who are watching. Sometimes when people get caught doing something wrong, they cry because they feel bad about what they did. Others in this situation cry because they feel bad that they were caught. Someone may be crying for reasons other than those associated with depression.

In other cases, people who are depressed may hide their sadness when they are in public. They may look like the life of the party, but when they go home their smiles are gone and the hollowness within them returns. Rather than admitting that there is something wrong, many people who are depressed cover up their feelings in public only to return to the anguish of their lives when they are alone. They do not realize that there is a better way to live.

What is common across the different faces of depression is not an expression but a feeling of deep sadness that does not go away. As a result, you cannot just look at someone and know whether he or she is depressed or just sad because of some serious loss or life event.

Additionally, the language that we use to describe depression makes it difficult to communicate what is being experienced. Very often, people do not have the words to say what they are feeling and end up using words and expressions that understate or misrepresent what they are experiencing. They may say, "I feel sad," when a more accurate statement would be "I don't enjoy anything in my life."

Moreover, some people who have had lifelong depression have learned to cope with their depression by learning how to hide what they feel from others. But coping is not a lifelong strategy. It is best used in the short term while a more permanent long-term solution is developed so that you are able to return to enjoying your life.

Developing a long-term life strategy means more than coming up with a long to-do list. In fact, just making up such a list can exacerbate depression. You may feel overwhelmed by all the things you have to do because you do not have the energy to do even a few of them.

In our culture there are core beliefs that drive what we value and what we do. While these are the values that can make you happy and successful, they also can be taken to an extreme, making you feel bad. When it comes to depression, these values can be distorted to the point where it is unlikely that a person can take the steps to address the depression in his or her life.

This is problematic because depression is pervasive in all communities and we need to treat it. Since practically everyone knows someone who is either depressed or has had to care for someone with depression, there has been much progress made in reducing the stigma associated with depression. The once-powerful stigma based on cultural taboos has been replaced by more of a reluctance, especially among Hispanics, to admit that that they are depressed.

Work, endurance, and family

Many Hispanics hesitate to admit that they suffer from depression because depression is inconsistent with their core beliefs and values. Our values about work, endurance, and family can create barriers to overcoming depression and living a happier life.

WORK

THE IMPORTANCE OF WORK IN DEFINING A PERSON IS INHERENT IN OUR culture. Just as clear is the importance of working hard. If, for some reason, you cannot work and there is nothing that is visibly wrong with you, then you are viewed in a negative way. For Hispanics, this need to work and produce is even more pronounced than it is among most other groups. Even stronger are the negative consequences when someone does not work. Hispanics will say the person is *flojo* or *vago*, and while that translates into English as "lazy," the connotation is much more negative. As a result, the healthy and good drive to work prompts people to hide their depression because they do not want to admit that they cannot work, so they suffer through each day in the workplace.

The sense of self-worth based on the work we do is also an important part of our mental well-being. When you are depressed, oftentimes you are unable to work or to work well. You may have trouble concentrating, remembering, or staying focused. When the depression is severe, you may be unable to work at all and may call in sick without being able to truthfully report the medical condition that kept you home. To make matters worse, people are often concerned that if they admit in the workplace that they have depression, all their work will be considered suspect because their problem is "in their head."

This is how the strong work ethic, which is a defining part of Hispanic culture, can also reduce our capacity to accept and recognize that there are those who cannot work because their life is framed by depression. Our strong work ethic complicates the situation because people may not want to talk about their experiences with depression or seek treatment. As a result, people with depression tend to reveal very little about their condition because they feel that it is better to hide what they are experiencing. All they can do is hope that they can get through the day and that perhaps the depression will go away. Too many people do this, and it is a part of what makes depression so difficult to address.

ENDURANCE

WHETHER IT IS THE FEMININE OR MASCULINE CONCEPT OF KEEPING A "stiff upper lip"—*aguantando* or *machismo*—the cultural message is the same. In order to be respected, you have to accept whatever is happening in your life. We communicate this to everyone in many ways, across all ages and both genders.

When children and adolescents describe their sadness, we do not listen as intently as we should because the tendency is to play down their concerns as if young people could not possibly have any problems at their age. When teens are irritable, we dismiss it as just part of being a teenager and do not realize that if those feelings last for longer than a year professional help may be required. We are likely to tell children to "just get over it" because we do not recognize their pain. The reality is that children also suffer from their losses, from low self-esteem, and even with depression. And while we may ignore what children and adolescents experience, we also encourage adults to ignore their own experiences. This is especially true in the Hispanic community.

Latinas are still socialized to *aguantar* (endure) and not discuss whatever negative feelings they are having. We send the message that the proper response is simply for them to handle things, not complain, and just keep going. If you had a baby, you are supposed to be happy. If you are not, then you have to be quiet about it and just go back to doing your work. Rarely do women hear about the high rate of depression among women after pregnancy (postpartum depression). *Aguantar* means that, even if you are suffering, you do not admit it and you do not seek help.

> Julio mentioned that it was good to be with the other guys in his new company because they just got the job done. They each came with a specific idea in mind and tried to make it work. Some liked the company, others were less enthusiastic about it, but none seemed to have much angst. I reminded him that men do not talk to other men about their angst. Julio's response was silence. In his silence he affirmed what I had just said. Men do not talk about their feelings—least of all to other men.

Just as stifling as *aguantar* is for Latinas, Hispanic men know that, in some ways, they still resonate to the strands of *machismo*, which were the norm in the past. The good part of *machismo* is that it makes a man feel responsible for taking care of his family. The burden of *machismo* is that you have to be strong and powerful and can never show feelings of sadness, since that would be a sign of weakness. As a result, Hispanic men are uncomfortable talking about their feelings and do whatever they can to block out the feelings associated with depression.

These strong cultural messages can be taken to an extreme that creates unintended negative consequences. And while the cultural values of *aguantando* and *machismo* may have produced some good outcomes, they can be misapplied and make life unbearable.

This is particularly true for young people who are coming to terms with their own sexual identity. Gay youth are two to three times more likely to attempt suicide than other youth. This risk drops dramatically in a supportive environment. Gender roles are complex messengers of what the culture values, and depression results when people know who they are and recognize the barriers that their sexual identity creates for them.

The important messages here include that it is not healthy (1) for Latinas to believe that they have to accept whatever negative things come into their life, (2) for Hispanic men to believe that being a man means that you have to hide feelings of depression, and (3) for young people to believe that they cannot be true to themselves. Endurance is good but it needs to be tempered with a strong dose of prudence.

FAMILY

THE IMPORTANCE OF FAMILY (BLOOD RELATIVES OR NOT) AND OF BEING connected to others is well documented. The extended family helps communities throughout the world survive through difficult times and helps us to celebrate all the events in our lives. The value of family as a source of support and nurturance is essential to all societies.

We also know that many more families than we would like to admit do not cultivate the kind of environment that fosters healthy relationships. This becomes a problem when the family colludes to cover up when things are wrong and, by doing so, encourages unhealthy behavior. In these families, people only seek help from family members and never ask anyone else for help because they would have to reveal that there is a problem.

> Hortensia sent an invitation to her children, their spouses, and her grandchildren to get together for a dinner at her house. She had come from a large family and was looking forward to the family gathering. Hortensia was surprised and hurt when several members of the family made it clear that they did not want to come to the get-together. She had not realized there were any real problems. She chose to ignore the depression, the lies, the alcoholism, the abuse, and the court battles that had pitted them against one another.

Some people spin fantasies about the relationships they have with members of their family in order to make believe that everything is fine. That is why, when someone in a family has depression, too often how the family handles it may be part of the problem. In such families, individuals ignore or pretend that there are no problems and, as a result, sometimes end up making matters worse for everyone. That is why it is important to encourage everyone to talk about depression and mental wellness in different settings.

No family can handle depression on their own, nor should they feel that they have to. That is why we must talk about depression and seek help outside the family. While the family can be helpful, there are limits to what any one member can do. The challenge is to use the strength that families can bring to an individual with the treatment options that are best for the type of depression that is experienced. Being able to talk about depression means taking the positive aspects of our values regarding work, endurance, and family into a therapeutic dimension. Talking about depression is the first step on the path to getting better.

When I am talking to a group about health, in addition to addressing major physical health concerns, I also ask questions related to personal well-being and, more directly, about audience members' experiences with depression. Although most people are willing to talk about physical ailments like diabetes and heart disease, when I ask about depression the atmosphere in the room changes. There is usually an uneasy pause in the discussion.

I watch as people look at each other. What usually happens next is that a woman in the group will begin by hesitantly talking about an experience she had with depression. The other women will listen intently. Most of the men will be silent and some will go so far as to avoid eye contact because they do not want to be drawn into the discussion. At times like these it is clear that there are still differences in how easily men and women can talk about their feelings.

Research has shown that women are socialized to be more attuned to their feelings, know better how to express them, and also know that in some situations it is acceptable for them to talk about conditions like depression. For men the situation is altogether different. Too often men who experience depression are silent about their experience because they do not have the words to describe either their feelings or what is going on inside them. Men may experience lots of distress and, because those feelings are the ones that they are not supposed to experience or reveal, they feel that they have to do whatever they can to tamp them down. Without a healthy outlet for those feelings of depression, some men—and, increasingly, some younger Latinas—drink excessive amounts of alcohol or abuse other drugs to cover-up the feelings of depression that permeate their lives.

Throughout our communities there is much suffering that is ignored or hidden because we do not know how to talk about deeply personal and emotional topics. This is compounded by the common but incorrect belief that being depressed is a matter of personal choice. No one chooses to be miserable.

Too many men, women, and children lead lives that could be happier if they knew that they had a condition for which there was treatment. To help all of us, we have to stop using language that either minimizes the seriousness of depression or diminishes and blames the people who struggle with this condition every day of their lives.

Understanding the signs

Part of the problem with our understanding of depression is that we use the word to cover a broad range of experiences. Sometimes, when we are sad, we use the word depressed to describe how we feel and confuse that with depression. Depression is much more than the sadness you feel because you did not get the phone call you expected or the gift you wanted.

Being sad and staying sad for weeks at a time can be a sign of a more serious situation. Feeling unhappy is different from the major depression that you may experience once in your life or that is a recurring event that exhausts your emotional resources and creates a vacuum that consumes all hope and breeds despair. Depression drains those who experience it and the people closest to them of the energy to do what they need to do to get better.

Over time, depression distorts more and more aspects of a person's life as the negative feelings and the inability to get things done become embedded in his or her life. The person who is severely depressed experiences a profound sadness that overwhelms and immobilizes his or her life.

Understanding the depth of depression and the importance of moving forward also means that we cannot let ourselves be misled by stereotypes in the media that portray depression as something found only among affluent non-Hispanic whites. In fact, the data show that Hispanics, African-Americans, and Asian Americans are more likely to experience depression than are non-Hispanic whites.

Depression is found in all communities. It is so common that each year 1 in 15 people has a major depressive disorder.

Since health is about the wellness of the body, mind, and spirit, it is important to use that framework to understand what we are experiencing so that we can take the necessary steps to get better. The signs and symptoms of depression available from the National Institute of Mental Health are described below in clusters that are consistent with a more comprehensive view of depression. The list includes unintended changes in how the body functions, when the mind is not working as well as it has in the past, and when the spirit feels diminished and burdened with life. If you have some or all of the symptoms listed below for more than two weeks and you have no physical illness to account for them, then you need to consider seeking professional help.

BODY (UNINTENDED CHANGES)

SLEEP

You are no longer able to sleep the way you used to. The number of hours you sleep is different or the quality of your sleep has changed. You may sleep more hours or you may find that you can only sleep for a few hours at a time. It may be difficult for you to go to sleep or to stay asleep.

FOOD

The amount of food you eat has changed, even though you did not intend to change it. You may eat a lot more than usual or you may eat a lot less. Be aware if you experience a change in weight that was unintended. Some people with depression gain weight and some lose weight.

PAIN

Your body may not feel good. You may have ongoing aches and pains, headaches, cramps, or digestive problems that do not go away.

MIND (NOT WORKING WELL)

ANXIETY

Your mind is not at rest. At different times you may feel sad, anxious, or even as if you have no feelings at all.

GROUCHINESS

You have a short temper and find that you get annoyed easily. Sometimes you have difficulty being in one place and have a need to move around.

NO JOY

It is hard to find anything to do that will give you pleasure. Even the things that you liked to do no longer seem enjoyable, including sexual intimacy.

UNCLEAR

You are not able to think the way you once did. You cannot focus on anything, the details are lost, your thoughts get muddled, and, when given choices, you have trouble deciding what you want to do. Trying to make a decision is difficult.

SPIRIT (DIMINISHED)

NO ENERGY
You do not have the energy to do anything.

HOPELESS
You feel that hope has vanished from your life and that life will not get better.

UNWORTHY
You feel that things that have gone awry in your life are your fault, that you are not worthy of anything good in life, or that there is nothing you can do to make your life situation better.

DEATH
You have thought about ending your life or actually tried to end your life.

Depression can be found in all communities, and it may occur at any point in a person's life. The consequences of teenage depression are something that should concern us all. Every year more Latinas under 18 attempt suicide than any other group of girls. This should be unacceptable and yet those numbers have been the same for nearly 15 years. One explanation for this high rate of attempted suicide by young Latinas is that, regardless of family income or whether the family had insurance, Hispanic teens are less likely than non-Hispanic white teens to either get medication for the treatment of major depression or to receive other mental health services.

At the other end of the spectrum, some of our older men and women have all the symptoms of depression but their symptoms are ignored. Instead, their suffering is attributed to getting older or being confused. If we spent more time with them, we might be surprised to find out that they are alone, no one is taking care of them, and that they are, in fact, clinically depressed. We have much to learn about depression across the ages.

To better understand depression, the Centers for Disease Control and Prevention (CDC) asked 235,067 adults to describe their experiences during the previous two weeks. The survey that was used was CDC's Behavioral Risk Factor Surveillance System, which CDC officials describe as the "world's largest, ongoing telephone health survey system, tracking health conditions and risk behaviors in the United States yearly since 1984."

The answers people gave indicated that in just the last two weeks, 1 out of 11 people met the criteria for current depression and that 1 in 30 met the criteria for major depression. What was revealing was that everybody did not have the same risk of experiencing depression. For example, women who were previously married or never married were more likely than married women to have current symptoms of depression. Hispanics, non-Hispanic blacks, and non-Hispanic people of other races were more likely to report major depression than non-Hispanic whites.

What is clear from this work is that depression is a common condition. Many more people described depressive symptoms than what was expected. The good news is that there are ways you can manage your life to reduce the likelihood that you will become depressed and, if you are diagnosed with depression, there is treatment.

The actual diagnosis of depression is difficult for many reasons. In addition to the many situations that fall under the broad umbrella of depression, the actual diagnosis is not as objective as reading an x-ray and diagnosing a broken bone. Determining if what a person is experiencing is depression takes time, experience, and good clinical judgment.

Most mental health care providers use the American Psychiatric Association's Diagnostic and Statistical Manual (DSM) as a guide for diagnosis and potential treatment. DSM also provides a framework to report information to insurance companies on the specific conditions that are being treated. The manual covers mental health conditions for children and adults. The most recent edition (DSM-IV) was published in 1994, with only some text revisions in 2000. Since then, many work groups were formed to update the DSM and to make it consistent with current science. An updated edition (DSM-V) is expected to be published in May 2013. Throughout the intervening years, the updating process has included input from thousands of professionals, patients, and researchers who have sent comments and research findings to help make the next edition a more relevant document.

In the area of depression, there have been many suggestions for changes based on the latest science and research findings. One recommendation is to increase the importance of anxiety as part of the clinical picture of depression. Another is for the manual to include bereavement-related depression as an event that can trigger a major depressive episode. The issue provoking the most discussion is how to address dysthymic disorders (depression that is ongoing and lasts for years, but with symptoms not as severe as those of major depression). The current proposal is to rename dysthymia chronic depressive disorder.

All this may sound like an exercise in semantics, but the ramifications are very important because the diagnosis that is given is used to determine the most effective treatment options for the person. This is of great consequence, since no single intervention or medication will work in all cases, even when people are diagnosed with the same condition. The nuances of each person's life experiences and brain chemistry, combined with the resources at his or her disposal, help to determine which treatment options and life changes will lead to the best outcome.

There are some things science has confirmed, but they provide more of a general framework than specifics in how to address depression. According to the National Institute of Mental Health, part of the National Institutes of Health, for mild to moderate depression, psychotherapy may be the best treatment option. For more severe cases or for different age groups (adolescents or older adults, for example) the combination of medication and psychotherapy may provide the best results. What is left for the clinician and the patient to determine is the specific therapy and medication that will work for that particular patient.

Beyond feeling blue

I remember how I felt when my mother died. She was so young, only 67, and I still needed her so very much. My first feeling after she died was of excruciating pain in my jaw. I did not know where that came from and I went to see my internist. He told me that the reason my jaw hurt so very much was because, in all probability, for days I had been locking my jaw. He asked me if I was okay and I said yes. I had had to make so many decisions in the last 72 hours to try to keep Mom alive. It was more stressful to me than I had imagined. And then she was dead.

After she died, I could not sleep at night and, much to my surprise, without trying I lost 10 pounds in 3 weeks. I just could not eat. The thought of food was too much to bear and when I tried to eat I could not swallow; the food seemed to get stuck in my throat. I did not want to hear music because it stirred my emotions and I could not tolerate that. Even looking at clothes in my favorite color—red—seemed like too much stimulation for my senses. My red sweaters seemed to screech out to me when I saw them. It was too intense to look at them, so I folded them up and put them away.

It was at that moment that I recognized that I had the symptoms of depression and decided that I should see a mental health professional to make sure that I would be okay.

Most of us would say that when people are depressed they are sad or crying all the time. The reality is that, in most cases, someone with depression is not sad all the time; sometimes such a person may appear to be grouchy, very restless, or even happy.

Keep in mind that we use the terms *depression* and *depressed* to cover many different situations, a number of which do not fall under the heading of clinical depression. For most people, the term *depressed* indicates when someone is sad or grieving or has had a bad day. At times, however, the sadness is considered typical and expected. For example, when you suffer a loss, it is expected that you will feel sadness; in fact, it would be cause for concern if you did not feel sad. If a loved one died and you were not sad, you would be considered insensitive, callous, or even odd. But depression is different than being sad. It is a feeling that is beyond grief and lasts a lot longer.

Depression is also difficult to accurately diagnose because it is based on what we say. In the best of circumstances, we often do not have either the words or the ease in expressing ourselves to explain our feelings very well. When we are depressed, it becomes even more difficult to find the words to articulate the experience. This is another factor that makes the diagnosis of depression challenging.

For most health problems, getting a diagnosis is straightforward. When you are diagnosed with high blood pressure or diabetes, it is because the readings your health care provider took were too high. Based on those test results, your health care provider will give you medicines to take, recommend changes to make in your lifestyle, and have you monitor your blood sugar level or blood pressure regularly.

For depression, there is no single objective test or measure to determine when a person is depressed. There are questions that can be asked and written tests that can be given, but in order to come up with an accurate diagnosis, the person must be able to understand the questions, be able to answer the questions, and feel comfortable answering the questions honestly. Trying to determine if someone has depression is difficult because communication is at the root of being able to make an accurate diagnosis.

For Hispanics, diagnosis is even more complicated because issues of language and culture are intertwined with how we describe what and how we feel. The words we use to describe our despair are often muted when we try to translate what we experience into English. Moreover, our belief that we should not complain about what is wrong, but instead endure whatever unpleasantness we are experiencing, makes it even harder for us to acknowledge that what is wrong needs treatment and care.

Getting an accurate diagnosis is complicated because sometimes the symptoms of depression are similar to the symptoms of many physical conditions (such as generalized aches and pains, headaches, stomach problems, and the like). Diagnosing depression becomes even more complicated for women and Hispanics because research shows that when physical symptoms are reported by members of these groups, too often they are either ignored or dismissed. Additionally, diagnosis of depression is difficult because, depending on your age (from children to older adult) and gender, you may experience a variety of symptoms, based on your life situation or the events that frame the depression.

TYPES OF DEPRESSION

DEPRESSION IS A MOOD DISORDER THAT ENCOMPASSES SEVERAL TYPES OF conditions. These conditions may vary from one person to another, based on the person's age, gender, cultural expectations and values, and by what is going on in that person's life that may have triggered the episode. The National Institute for Mental Health (NIMH) assigns a different name to each type of depression, depending on how severe it is (from major depression to dysthymia); when it occurs, for example, after having a baby (postpartum depression) or when there is a season with less natural sunlight (seasonal affective disorder [SAD]); or by the severity of other symptoms (bipolar disorder or psychotic depression). The NIMH designations are similar to those found in the DSM, although there are some differences. The information below is designed to serve as a guide to give you a better appreciation of the range of conditions and some of their defining characteristics.

MAJOR DEPRESSIVE DISORDER

When you have a *major depressive disorder*, also called major depression, your relationships with others, your family life, your work, and the pleasurable aspects of your life seem to grind to a halt, and you cannot do nor want to do the things you normally would do. In this situation, people lack the energy and desire to move forward in their life. For some people this type of major depression may occur once in their life (single episode), while for others it may occur at different points in their lives (recurrent).

Anna and Edgar were known among their family and friends as a very hardworking couple. They always seemed to be on the go and getting things done. Anna was busy trying to help people learn new skills while Edgar put in long hours at his small business. Their marriage of many years had grown from the friendship that had brought them together. And yet when Anna looked at Edgar she saw a man who seemed different than the one she had married; sometimes he even seemed anxious. Over the years Anna felt an increasing heaviness in their lives that she did not understand. Those were usually the times when Edgar would get anxious and was not even interested in being sexually intimate. One night when they were having dinner, Edgar looked at her and blurted out, "I am so depressed and have been that way all of my life." Anna was astonished and responded, "How could that be? I never saw you being sad or crying and we have been together for a long time." And as the tears welled up in his eyes he continued to look down at his plate and said, "You are not with me all day. I have been depressed all my life ... it has been that way all of my life ... I just learned how to hide it."

DYSTHYMIA

When the symptoms of depression seem mild and last a long time a person may have *dysthymia* or *chronic depressive disorder* (the term proposed for DSM-V). In this case, he or she has a depressed mood on most days, has felt that way for at least two years, and two months have never gone by without these feelings of sadness. In children and teens, the feelings have to last for at least one year and may also include being irritable. Although it may not be as severe as major depression, dysthymia usually lasts longer. Dysthymia is sometimes difficult to diagnose because what a person experiences is not as disabling as in a major depressive disorder. At times, a person is able to do some of what he or she has to do, even though the negative feelings linger. Some people with dysthymia may also have episodes of major depression throughout their life.

POSTPARTUM DEPRESSION

In the Hispanic community, where larger families are more common and having children is celebrated, it is particularly difficult to accept that there is a type of depression that some mothers experience within six months of giving birth that is known as *postpartum depression*. This type of major depressive disorder is inconceivable for some because for most women, and especially so for Hispanics, having a baby is a time of great happiness. While that may be true in most cases, for 10–15 percent of women the period after giving birth is very difficult. This is a complicated time for these women because the many changes in their lives and all the adjustments that have to be made by adding another member to the family are overwhelming. At the same time, the hormones in their body are going through major fluctuations and compromising their emotional stability.

SEASONAL AFFECTIVE DISORDER (SAD)

Alberto was busy all summer long. He would get up early and go out to work. Each day brought new challenges and hard physical labor. Alberto would laugh with the crew and sometimes he would even bring a special lunch to share with the other guys. As fall came, the work changed and he had to be indoors more. He found that he wasn't sleeping as well and he had started to add those extra pounds he attributed to the winter. As the nights grew longer, it got harder for him to focus on the work he had to do and he found that he was easily distracted. Alberto still was doing the same kind of work but he was enjoying it less, and every day it seemed to get tougher for him to get up and go to work. He just didn't want to get out of bed.

When Ileana told me about her husband, I could only imagine how hard her life had been. While their family and friends saw them as the perfect couple, Ileana knew that their life was a lot more complicated than it appeared. Every winter, especially around the holidays, José would become moody. As the days progressed, those moods would give way to a depression that would make it impossible for him to enjoy the life they had built together. José would just get lost in the fog that seemed to envelop his mind. Ileana felt helpless as she watched the man she loved drown in his winter depression once again.

People with *seasonal affective disorder* find that as the natural sunlight decreases in the winter, the symptoms of their depression increase. This is a major depressive disorder in which we know that light plays a critical role. Although light has been identified as a key trigger for SAD, only half the people with SAD respond to light therapy alone.

OTHER TYPES OF CONDITIONS THAT INCLUDE DEPRESSION

There are also individuals who seem to go through major emotional ups and downs that are not connected to events in their life. When this occurs, the person may be said to have a *bipolar disorder* or a *manic-depressive* condition. The use of the word *manic* describes cycles when the person appears very busy, and engages in lots of activities, but is not productive. The number of people with bipolar disorder seems to be increasing. It is estimated that for 50–66 percent of adults with a bipolar disorder, the illness began before they were 19 years old. People with *psychotic depression may* have hallucinations or delusions, in addition to the behaviors that are found with depression. Bipolar disorder and psychotic depression are less common than dysthymia or major depression.

While these descriptions provide some information there are differences from one person to another. Obtaining a professional diagnosis is essential so that you can get the treatment that will produce the best outcomes for you.

DEPRESSION AND ITS RELATIONSHIP TO OTHER HEALTH CONCERNS

The key challenge is to care for all of our health conditions. In most circumstances, getting better requires us to do something and being depressed makes it harder to do the things we want to and should do. So most health care providers know that they have to treat depression along with whatever other conditions are present.

The relationship between depression and other ongoing health conditions has been well documented. We know that if you have diabetes, for instance, you are more likely to also have depression. The same is also true for people with heart problems.

DIABETES

If you have type 2 diabetes and depression, you may wonder whether one condition caused the other. Depression may increase the likelihood of having type 2 diabetes, but it is also true that having type 2 diabetes increases the likelihood that you will be diagnosed with depression. It is not known if one causes the other. One possible reason that women who have depressive symptoms are at increased risk for diabetes may be due to the link between stress and depression. As a woman's body produces more cortisol—the hormone associated with stress—her belly fat increases. Belly fat is a risk factor for metabolic syndrome—one of the conditions that increases the likelihood of getting diabetes. It is interesting to note that while men who are under stress also produce cortisol, they do not get the belly fat.

CORONARY HEART DISEASE (CHD)

If you have coronary heart disease, you are three times more likely to be diagnosed with depression than someone without CHD. Depressive symptoms also increase the likelihood that someone with a broad range of heart problems will have a heart attack or have to be hospitalized for heart problems. So it is essential to manage the depressive symptoms of people with conditions that can involve sudden reduced blood flow to the heart.

Some of the hormones related to stress—which can be a precursor to depression—may have an impact on the heart as well. What is still unclear is whether depression actually causes a heart problem. The two are definitely related, however, and health care providers must focus on treating both conditions. It may be that some of the hormones related to stress also have an impact on the heart. While we do not have all the facts you can be certain that chronic psychological stress is not good for your heart.

Stress is a problem for people of all ages. A study that looked at teens (adolescents) found that even when you took into consideration the differences in weight, income, education, and life events, those teens who reported that they had more daily interpersonal stress had higher levels of a protein (called C-reactive protein) that is associated with inflammation and cardiovascular problems. Similarly, people—especially men—who hid their anger and who harbored hostility compromised the health of their heart. Even when the mental stress was experimentally induced, people with cardiovascular disease were more likely to produce substances that were harmful to their hearts.

In a study of 215 healthy adults, it was documented that as we get older depression seems to have an impact on the health of our heart in different ways. The researchers used the Personal Well-Being Index to determine which people had depressive symptoms. The findings indicate that the depressive symptoms in older men seemed to compromise the way the heart works, more so than for older women.

Regardless of the type of heart problem someone experiences (coronary heart disease, unstable angina, heart attack, heart failure, recuperation from coronary bypass surgery), researchers have found that 15–20 percent of those with a heart problem have a major depressive disorder. Additionally, there is a larger group who show signs of milder depression. This is important to take into account for the full recovery of a person after a cardiac event.

In addition to diabetes and heart disease, there is a link between depression and a range of other conditions. For example, Hispanics with rheumatoid arthritis—especially more recent arrivals in the United States—are more likely to have symptoms of depression and psychological distress than non-Hispanics. What remains unknown is whether the depression caused each condition or the conditions caused the depression. Regardless of which came first, when you are diagnosed with depression it is more difficult to do the things you need to do to take care of yourself.

Whether people have been diagnosed with diabetes or HIV, their ability to follow through on their own care is reduced when they are also diagnosed with depression. There are bits of information emerging to help us better understand and care for ourselves. One thing is certain—having the additional diagnosis of depression increases the likelihood that you will have an unfavorable outcome.

Regardless of the type of depression or other health conditions that people may have, they need to take action based on the instructions they receive from their health care provider. When you begin to implement your treatment plan, you may feel as if you are dragging yourself to do what you know you must do, but sometimes that is the only way to start.

The biology of depression

I never knew that depression was an illness. —Leonor

Our thoughts, feelings, and behaviors are complex. Understanding what makes them unique for each one of us means that we have to look at all the parts that make us do whatever we do. We have genes that predispose us to or protect us from illness, cells that make up our brain structure, and biochemistry in our brain and body. We also interact with the external environment, which affects everything. To understand what you can do to overcome depression, it is helpful to know more about the biology of depression.

GENES

YOUR BODY HAS ABOUT 10 TRILLION CELLS. IN THE CENTER OF EACH cell, there are threadlike structures (chromosomes) that carry your genes. Your genes have the DNA (deoxyribonucleic acid) that you inherited from your parents. Most DNA is found in the center (nucleus) of each cell; this is called nuclear DNA. A small amount of DNA can also be found in other parts of the cell (mitochondrial DNA).

Genes are the pieces of DNA that have the instructions for creating every part of your body. Each cell has about 20,000 genes. All these pieces working together are part of what makes you who you are. We are still learning a lot about our genes.

Mapping the human genome was supposed to open a new understanding for many conditions, including depression. That is why, beginning in 2003, there was a big push to try to identify and sort out a depression gene. It was hoped that genes would help identify who would be at risk for depression. As the research continued, it became evident that only a few very rare diseases were caused by a specific gene.

At this point what we know is that there is no single gene that causes depression. While a particular gene for depression has not been discovered, researchers found that people who had a short version of a particular gene (5-HTTLPR), as opposed to the longer version, were more likely to develop depression when faced with stress. Research is under way to identify other genes that may also have an impact on depression.

Even parts of the material in each of your cells play an important role in the genesis of depression. Telomeres, which are located at the end of chromosomes, block the chromosome from combining inappropriately and they also seem to protect the chromosomes from attack. As we age, our telomeres get shorter. Psychological stress, which for some people is a known trigger for depression, is associated with accelerating the shortening of telomeres. At this point, early research suggests that some of the factors that are likely to maintain the length of telomeres are: exercise; some medications given to treat depression (SSRIs or selective serotonin reuptake inhibitors); foods rich in omega-3 fatty acids and antioxidants; and stress-reduction techniques.

Information about genes may help determine which of the available treatments will work for a particular person. In some cases a gene may make it less likely or more likely that a medication will be effective. Genes have an effect on how drugs act, whether our body absorbs a drug slowly or quickly, and even how information is processed in the brain. This area of research is called pharmacogenetics. Some of the benefits and side effects from medications to treat depression are probably due to variability in the genes from one person to another.

In addition to understanding what is happening inside a cell, there is growing interest in the environmental and other factors that affect genes. In this type of research the focus is on external factors that turn genes on or off, or change how they function. For example, there is strong evidence that smoking has an impact on genes and how we metabolize drugs. Additionally, some provocative research in behavioral epigenetics (the study of how life experiences may change genes) suggests that early life experiences can have a major impact on some selected genes.

And while some want to say that your genes tell the entire story of who you are, there are those who think otherwise. Take the example of identical twins. At first you may have difficulty telling them apart, but the longer you are with them the more you can see the differences between them in terms of their emotional responses and facial expressions. What we learn from twin studies is that even identical genetic code does not produce identical behaviors. This is because experience and environment are essential factors in shaping our behavior.

Genes are important in determining how well a person can adapt to his or her environment but how that adaptation happens is still unclear. While your genes and the experiences you have interact, we still need to understand how that results in changes in our behavior. Stress actually changes (that is, it leaves methyl marks on) your DNA and can have an impact throughout your life. Suffice it to say that we have a long way to go before we fully grasp the connection between our genes and depression. It is hoped that the next decade of research will provide the valuable information we need to understand the role of genes in depression.

BRAIN

THE BRAIN IS PART OF THE CENTRAL NERVOUS SYSTEM. IT IS ONE OF THE major control centers for your body and how it works determines how well you interact with everything around you. Your brain is the source of most of your feelings and thoughts. The information your senses gather is processed there, behavior is initiated and controlled there, and emotions are born there.

The brain has three parts—the hindbrain, the midbrain, and the forebrain. The hindbrain (upper part of the spinal cord, brain stem, and cerebellum) controls body functions that you do not have to think about (breathing and heart rate, for example). This part of the brain also includes the cerebellum, which gives you balance and the ability to coordinate your movements. The midbrain controls some reflexes as well as voluntary movements, including eye movement.

The forebrain, the largest part of the brain, includes the cerebrum and those parts of the brain most associated with feelings, perceptions, and responses. The frontal lobes are responsible for a person's executive functions. This refers to your ability to plan, reason, have abstract thoughts, and exercise self-control. The forebrain also includes other structures, such as the hypothalamus, the thalamus, the hippocampus, and the amygdala. The hypothalamus is the size of an almond and controls the molecules that make you feel exhilarated, angry, or unhappy. It also links the nervous system to the endocrine system through the pituitary gland. The thalamus relays information to the other parts of the brain, while the hippocampus has a role in memory and more complex cognitive functions.

The role of the amygdala in depression is under increasing investigation. The amygdala is your personal gatekeeper, responsible for processing and recalling emotional reactions. Your "gut reaction" is believed to be the product of the amygdala. Recent research indicates that, regardless of gender or age, people with a larger amygdala reported having larger and more complex social networks. What the study did not address was whether a person with a larger amygdala is better able to form complex relationships or whether having the complex relationships makes the amygdala get larger.

The brain has many kinds of cells, but the most important ones are the neurons. Whatever you think or feel results from signals that pass from one neuron to the next. Sometimes there is a problem in the area between neurons (called the synapse) that makes it difficult to transmit the information from one to another. These problems may be due to chemicals, known as neurotransmitters, that are released by the tiny sacs at the end of the neuron or are present in the synapse so that the neurons can work well. Examples of these chemicals are serotonin, GABA (gamma-aminobutyric acid), acetylcholine, and dopamine.

The role of serotonin with respect to depression is very complex. It seems that people who have depression do not have the proper amount of this neurotransmitter. Some have too much and others have too little. At present there is no test that can easily determine how much serotonin needs to be available.

When Congress declared the 1990s to be the Decade of the Brain, there was great hope that many questions would be answered. What we learned was that there was much research that still needed to be done to understand the structure and processes of the brain. The National Institute of Neurological Disorders and Stroke, part of the National Institutes of Health, supports research on over 600 neurological diseases and the National Institute of Mental Health (NIMH), also part of NIH, is doing other research to clarify the relationship between the brain and our behavior.

Our research on the brain and how it functions has been advanced by our ability to use brain scans to measure the structure of the brain, blood flow, and levels of oxygen and glucose. While brain scans are not a tool for diagnosis, the new information they provide has helped to revise and expand what we know about the brain.

The adult brain is a structure that has the ability to change how it works as a result of experience. This is called neuroplasticity, and it is important because it means that the brain can change.

Cultural neuroscience is a growing area of investigation that tries to explain how culture influences the ways in which the brain develops. It is not that a brain from one culture is better than a brain from another but, rather, that there are differences from culture to culture in how people process information. Some studies have compared American and Chinese brain function and documented differences between them. There is little that is known about other communities.

Brain activity, as measured by existing technology, does not give us clear-cut answers. While being in love, having a drug addiction, or being obsessive-compulsive are different, brain scans have shown that the brains of those in love, drug-addicted, or obsessive-compulsive all look the same. Based on brain scans, it seems that over time couples often develop powerful feelings of attachment that replace those of romantic love. But when couples do new things together that they both enjoy, it seems to trigger the "romantic love" image of the brain. What is certain is that what the picture of your brain means can change based on the situation; it may also be very similar to the brain scans of people in very different settings.

We are also learning more about how stress affects the brain. Stress upsets the normal interaction between the hypothalamus, the pituitary gland, and the adrenal glands. When the communication between these glands is no longer synchronized, a person is more likely to have depressive symptoms. In addition, researchers have determined that men and women react to stress in different ways.

There are many challenges that remain. We are still learning about how to measure the brain, how to interpret the images of the brain, and what factors can change how the brain works. All this new information needs to be carefully analyzed to determine the impact that changes in how the brain functions has on depression.

HORMONES

THE IMPACT OF HORMONES ON WHAT WE ARE THINKING AND WHAT WE are feeling has been getting increased attention in recent years. We know that during adolescence and, later in life, during menopause that changes in hormones cause a shift in mood. When it comes to our feelings and our ability to think, both estrogen and testosterone play significant roles.

There has been some research on how hormones affect women's moods. Research has shown that, during the first two years after menopause, there is a greater risk of having a major depressive episode. It is unclear whether this is due to hormonal changes or life events.

While researchers have been investigating the period when women are in their late 40s to early 50s, because this is a time of hormonal change for them, few studies probe the hormonal changes that men experience during this same time of life. The data on men should make us pause. Men who had decreased levels of testosterone had increased levels of depression and anxiety. This is also a time when men are more likely to commit suicide.

OXYTOCIN

Another hormone that has drawn interest among health researchers and the general public is oxytocin. This hormone, sometimes referred to as the "cuddle hormone," has received popular attention because it seems to have an impact on how people relate to one another. In particular, the number of studies on oxytocin in publications on psychology increased from 17 in 1990 to 118 by 2010. Much work needs to be done to determine whether oxytocin can be used as part of a treatment plan for depression. At this point there is strong evidence that this hormone reduces the stress responses in animals. Research with people is in the early stages and is at best suggestive.

CORTISOL

The role of cortisol in depression is pivotal because cortisol is the hormone associated with how we handle stress. Like stress itself, cortisol has a good side and a not-so-good side. Cortisol can prepare you for challenges but too much of it can cause all sorts of complications. Likewise, stress can increase your alertness but prolonged stress can lead to the unresolved anxiety that can morph into depression.

When you are in a stressful situation, cortisol is one of the chemicals your body releases to prepare your immune system to respond to the stress. After the stressful situation has passed, cortisol communicates to your immune system that it can relax. When you have too much stress in your life, cortisol just stays in your system and the cells in your immune system stop responding. That is why you begin to have problems when your stress level stays high and your cortisol level does not go back to normal levels.

If you have depression, you have a brain dysfunction that can be attributed to your genes, your cells, your system for information processing in the brain, your individual experiences, your cognitions, your temperament, and all the factors in your environment. Depression may be due to one of these factors or some combination of them. We are just starting to learn how these factors affect the brain, and to document the differences in children and adults.

Life changes to consider: The 10-point program for health and wellness

As we have seen, depression covers a range of conditions that are triggered by a variety of factors, and there are a number of options available for its treatment. For certain there is no solution that will work in all instances. To overcome depression requires work that begins with having you become more thoughtful about your life and reorganizing yourself for wellness. You will have to rethink how you spend your time and all of your resources.

The following 10-Point Program for Health and Wellness applies all the scientific knowledge that we have accumulated to help you have the life that you want to have. That is the purpose of the 10-Point Program—not just to help you thrive, but also to protect your body, mind, and spirit from depression. The principles that underlie the 10-Point Program are a fundamental part of the *Buena Salud* series and build on the new research that focuses on the need for therapeutic lifestyle changes (TLC). In our 10-Point Program for Health and Wellness, TLC retains it common meaning of tender loving care as that is what we should do for ourselves and for others and adds another meaning—therapeutic lifestyle changes.

The evidence is clear. In order to live a healthier and happier life, these are steps that you have to take. The best place to start on the path to wellness is by doing a self-assessment of what things you are doing and not doing.

Look at the questions below, think about each statement, and then honestly answer it. A True response means that the statement is true at least 95 percent of the time or at least 19 out of 20 times.

1. I eat and drink for a healthy body. ☐True ☐False

2. I exercise at least 5 times a week. ☐True ☐False

3. I take all my medications. ☐True ☐False

4. I have a regular source of health care. ☐True ☐False

5. I stay away from smoke and other toxic substances. ☐True ☐False

6. I get enough sleep. ☐True ☐False

7. I have healthy relationships. ☐ True ☐False

8. I keep a journal of my health. ☐True ☐False

9. I cherish my spiritual life. ☐True ☐False

10. I know how to listen to my body. ☐True ☐False

Now it is time to think about your answers and what are the opportunities for you to adopt a more health-promoting lifestyle. I do not know anyone who would answer all the items True or all of them False. For most of us, the answers will be a combination of True and False. Because we are all working to be stronger and healthier than we already are, most of us will have more False responses than True ones.

The 10 Points can be broken down into core items and magnifiers. Core items—#1 through #4—are your "must-do items." As you read the sections below, you will learn the latest techniques for creating and maintaining positive outcomes in all these areas. We all know what to do, and the suggestions and tools specified below will help you set the stage to do them.

Magnifiers are items #5 through #10. These multiply and amplify the benefits of your core activities. When you do them, they boost the benefits of your core actions (#1–#4), and when you do not do them, they lessen the impact of those efforts.

To find your starting point, look at items to which you answered False. Read the sections below and choose at least one of the False answers that you will work to change to a True. When you make the decision to follow the steps below, you are moving toward a healthier you and making life changes to improve your physical, mental, and spiritual health.

1. EAT AND DRINK FOR A HEALTHY BODY

TRY TO KEEP IN MIND THE 3PS OF HEALTHY EATING: pleasure, portion, and process.

Pleasure

You need to think about what you eat and how you eat, while enjoying the flavors and textures. You cannot eat mindlessly because it is a waste of calories and money. You cannot eat because you are upset, although there is a place for "comfort foods." You need to eat for nourishment, energy, and to enjoy your food. If you eat without thinking, then you will not be giving your body the fuel it needs to function well and you will not be as healthy as you could be.

We drink because our bodies are mostly water and that is why it is important to drink what is good for us.

Portion

Portions should be the amount that is best for you, not necessarily what is served. When you buy packaged foods, and increasingly even when you order food from restaurants, there is nutritional information provided that you need to read. I cannot begin to tell you the number of times that I thought a small container of juice was one serving and when I read the label I discovered that it was two or more servings. The label is a guide, but what constitutes a portion for you is based on specific factors.

Assuming the same level of activity throughout your life, as you get older your portion sizes should get smaller. Also, as your activity level decreases, your portion sizes should get smaller. When you are trying to decide how large a portion is best for you, do not look at what other people are eating; put on your plate the amount that is right for you. It may be more or it may be less than others are consuming. Be aware of the serving size that you need to eat to feel full. At the same time, remember that if you eat more than your body needs, your food will turn into bulges in places where you would prefer not to have them. So stop when you are full.

But what does *full* mean? That is something many of us have to learn. As you eat, try to think of how full your stomach feels and rate your fullness on a scale of 1 to 10, with 1 being so hungry that you feel faint and 10 feeling stuffed like a sausage.

Your goal is know when you get to a 5 and not to exceed that point. You also need to make sure your body has enough fuel throughout the day. Eating more small meals throughout the day may help you keep up your energy level.

Process

To eat food that is best for your body, you should eat fewer processed foods. You know that foods that are less processed are better for your body. A recent study analyzed information from 3,486 people who, over a five-year period, ate either whole food (heavily loaded by vegetables, fruits, and fish) or processed food (heavily loaded with sweetened desserts, fried food, processed meat, refined grains, and high-fat dairy products). At the end of the five years, the group who ate more processed food were more prone to depression than those who ate more whole food. Regardless of whether it was the food or that they were thoughtful about what they ate, the important message for all of us is to eat less processed food. This does not mean that you can never have any processed food, only that the amount you consume has to be very limited.

Another way to think about what is good for you to eat is to *eat brown* (brown rice, whole-wheat pasta, whole-grain breads, and, yes, the occasional dark chocolate), *eat colorful* (tomatoes, beans, greens), and *avoid white* (sugar, salt, fat, white bread, white rice).

Loretta had been in the same job for many years. She loved her job because it gave her the opportunity to improve the lives of others. When she first started working, she was very productive and would get everything done. Her enthusiasm was visible. She was appreciated and valued. It was all she wanted. Then her life started to go through the typical changes life brings: One relationship ended, the children grew up, and Loretta started to have more time to herself. It became exhausting to do her work, but she learned that people on the job with whom she had nurtured relationships over the years would help her when she was going through a rough spot. After a while, others were providing more than just help; they were actually doing her work because they saw that she just was not able to do it. Loretta began coming to work later and later. She complained that she could not go to sleep and that she could not get up in the morning. What she did not share with others was that every night when she was alone she would have two to three drinks to take the edge off.

You need to think about what you are drinking and the amount of sugar, calories, and alcohol you're consuming. This is especially true with alcoholic drinks, where the definition of one drink is determined by which beverage you are actually drinking (for example, beer, wine, scotch, or rum), since the amount of alcohol in each drink varies. One drink is a 12-ounce bottle of beer, a 5-ounce glass of wine, or a 1½-ounce shot of hard liquor. Sometimes, when you order a "specialty drink," there are three or four different shots in one glass. So your one glass may actually be two or three drinks.

The greatest concern is that people who have depression are at risk of becoming alcohol-dependent. What may start as a way to self-medicate can end up with disastrous consequences. *Alcohol abuse* is when people drink to excess, but do not have a physical addiction. *Alcoholism* is when people have physical signs of addiction. At this point, even though the alcoholic's life may be unraveling, he or she cannot stop drinking. The combination of depression and alcoholism should be avoided. In general, those at risk for alcoholism are:

- Men who have 15 or more drinks a week.
- Women who have 12 or more drinks a week.
- Anyone who has 5 or more drinks per occasion at least once a week.

While the occasional drink may be okay, keep in mind that alcohol abuse can lead to alcoholism and make depression more difficult to treat.

2. EXERCISE FOR LIFE

THE MANY BENEFITS OF EXERCISING MAKE IT ESSENTIAL THAT WE engage in physical activity because it is so very, very good for our mental wellness. When it comes to depression there is very strong evidence that exercise is both good as a means of preventing illness and therapeutic. While exercise is good for everyone with depression, it is particularly beneficial for people who are taking medication, women with postpartum depression, and older adults. The explanations for these good outcomes range from the impact of exercise on levels of serotonin to the fact that people who engage in regular exercise find that their sleep improves.

Exercise is good for our muscles and bones as well as every other part of our body, including our brain.

To maximize the benefits in terms of decreasing our risk for depression, it is key that we engage in physical activity that we enjoy and that makes us feel good. While you may look at what others do for inspiration, you have to be realistic as to what you will be able to do. Does this mean that you have to run a marathon or compete in an Iron Man race? If you can do so in a healthy way, that is fine. But the majority of us need to find some physical activity that we can work into our daily lives. At this point you may feel that you do not have the free time to dedicate to hours of exercise. The good thing is that you do not have to. You can start by taking 10 minutes to exercise three times a day. Over time you will increase what you are able to do.

According to the Physical Activity Guidelines for Americans, the weekly goals for adults are at least one of the following:

- 150 minutes of moderate-intensity aerobic activity (brisk walking) and muscle strengthening 2 or more days that work all the major muscle groups (legs, hips, back, abdomen, chest, shoulders, and arms);
- 75 minutes of vigorous-intensity aerobic activity (jogging or running) and muscle strengthening 2 or more days that work all the major muscle groups (legs, hips, back, abdomen, chest, shoulders, and arms); or
- A combination of moderate and vigorous aerobic activity and muscle strengthening 2 or more days that work all the major muscle groups (legs, hips, back, abdomen, chest, shoulders, and arms).

The type of exercise you do will also vary. Most likely at different points in your life you will find that there are different things that you like to do. Perhaps when you are in your teens you like to play team sports and then later, when it gets harder to get a group together, you may choose to ride a bicycle or walk. Some of us may be lifelong dancers. Regardless, the purpose of activity is to stay as active as possible. That does not mean that you always have to do the same thing.

Too often we find women stretching and men lifting weights. For both men and women, the best physical activity will have variety and will engage every part of your body. This means we all need to move to build and sustain our endurance (cardio), enhance our flexibility (stretching), and gain strength (weights).

And when we exercise, we do it at the level which we find ourselves at right now. Too often people try to pick up a form of physical activity where they left off years before. The result is that they overdo it and injure themselves. You should not expect to immediately be at the same level where you left off. And, of course, before you start your exercise program, be sure to talk to your health care provider to determine whether there are special considerations you need to take into account.

Exercise is so good for us. Although we do not fully understand why it works so well to overcome depression, it certainly is something we need to make a part of our lives.

3. TAKE YOUR MEDICATIONS (PRESCRIPTION AND OVER-THE-COUNTER)

IF YOUR HEALTH CARE PROVIDER PRESCRIBED MEDICINES FOR YOU, THEN you need to take them. Let your health care provider know if your medicine is giving you side effects. Do not stop taking them until you and your health care provider discuss the ramifications of no longer taking the medicine. Be sure to talk to your health care provider about all the medicines, teas, supplements, and other products you consume and use to be healthy.

Also be clear about how to take the medications prescribed for you. Too often people fill their prescriptions and just look at how often to take them and how many or how much of each they are supposed to take. That is why medications come with instructions on what to do and what not to do. Be aware about the specific instructions on how to take your medicine, for example, with water or with or without food. Whatever the instructions are, make sure that you understand and follow them. If you do not understand how and when you are sup-posed to take your medication, ask the pharmacist. It is better to ask questions than for the medication not to work because you are taking it the wrong way.

If you are taking more than one medication, use whatever system works for you (notebook, app, or calendar) to keep track of when you take each of your medications. This will be useful information for you to know and to have for your next visit to your health care provider.

4.

HAVE A REGULAR SOURCE OF HEALTH CARE

YOUR HEALTH CARE PROVIDER NEEDS TO BE AWARE OF HOW YOU ARE feeling. Depression often occurs with other conditions (heart problems, diabetes, etc.), and you need to have a health care provider who understands your total health. This also means that you have a responsibility to tell your health care provider about all your medical issues. Going for wellness visits should be part of what you do to take care of yourself.

5.

STAY AWAY FROM SMOKE AND OTHER TOXIC SUBSTANCES

SMOKING IS BAD FOR YOU BECAUSE IT INTRODUCES A TOXIC CHEMICAL to every cell in your body and also interferes with the effectiveness of some medications. When you inhale smoke from a cigarette (regardless of whether you or someone else is smoking), or breathe in toxic substances, those substances enter your body through your lungs and are picked up by red blood cells that need oxygen and are taken to every cell in your body.

We are just starting to document how toxic substances in our daily environment are disrupting our endocrine and immune systems, both of which play an important role in our brain chemistry and depression. Some of these chemicals may trigger the changes in our brain that could lead to depression.

6. GET ENOUGH SLEEP

ACCORDING TO A SURVEY CONDUCTED BY THE NATIONAL SLEEP Foundation most people (60 percent) said that they experience a sleep problem every night or almost every night. This is not good. Some of us mistakenly believe that when we sleep our bodies are resting and not doing anything important. Quite the contrary. When you sleep, your body continues to perform important functions, even though you are in a different state of awareness. Key hormones are produced while you sleep; these are essential for your physical and mental health. When you do not get enough sleep or the proper sleep, you experience many negative consequences. For example, women are more likely to have low sexual desire or other sexual problems if they do not get adequate sleep.

How much sleep you actually need varies greatly by age (see chart on facing page). For most adults, 7 to 9 hours of sleep is enough. There is some evidence that, for most people, sleeping only 4 to 5 hours causes negative consequences in their body and brain chemistry.

Remember that when you do not sleep well, your entire body is thrown into a state of confusion because a healthy body functions on a regular 24-hour cycle of physical, mental, and behavioral changes that respond primarily to light and darkness. This regular cycle is called your circadian rhythm, and it is driven by the biological clocks throughout your body. These biological clocks are actually groupings of interacting molecules in cells throughout the body. Your brain coordinates all the body clocks so that they are in sync. When they are out of sync, you are more likely to have symptoms of depression.

RANGE OF SLEEP NEEDS VARIES BY AGE	
AGE	HOURS OF SLEEP NEEDED
Up to 2 months	12–18 hours
3–11 months	14–15 hours
12–36 months	12–14 hours
3–5 years old	11–13 hours
5–10 years old	10–11 hours
10–17 years old	8. 5–9. 25 hours
18 and older	7–9 hours

Source: National Sleep Foundation Website

Disturbed sleep is found in people who experience depression. It is not clear which comes first—the sleep disturbance or the depression. We also know that lack of sleep becomes a major risk factor for depression, especially for people who do shift or night work, because this type of work upsets the circadian rhythms. How much sleep someone needs varies according to many factors.

Recent findings suggest that how much light you are exposed to between dusk and when you go to sleep is very important. It seems that the artificial light from screens (television, computer, video games, cell phone, etc.), especially in the hour before you go to sleep, disrupts the production of hormones associated with sleep and upsets your circadian rhythms.

According to the National Sleep Foundation, there are specific things that you need to do to increase the likelihood that you get a good night's sleep:

THE BUENA SALUD GUIDE TO OVERCOMING DEPRESSION

- Set and keep a schedule for when you need to go to sleep and when you need to wake up.
- Be aware of the effect of light. In the morning, when you want to be awake, bright light is helpful but at night it should be avoided.
- Keep to a program of regular exercise.
- Before you go to sleep, get into your "sleep time" mode.
- As much as possible, create an area that is for sleeping and not for work or entertainment. Your sleep area should be a sanctuary for you. Sometimes this is as simple as covering your head with your sheet and making believe you hear a soothing sound.
- Keep a pad next to your bed. If you wake up because of worries, write them down, and tell yourself you can forget about them until morning.
- At night, when it is close to the time you want to go to sleep, avoid food and drinks with caffeine (this includes chocolate), large meals, and drinks with alcohol.
- If you are taking medications, either prescription medicine or self-prescribed over-the-counter products, talk to your health care provider to make sure that they are not compounding your sleep problems.
- Unless you work nights, do not take any late-afternoon or evening naps. The best way to nap is before 3:00 p. m. and for less than 45 minutes.

I also think that one of the other considerations that can help you to have better sleep is to be able to go to sleep and know that you have put in a good day's work, that you have done nothing to be hurtful to anyone else, and that perhaps what you did today helped someone else. People who can feel good about what they have done are able to sleep in way that is restful to the body and spirit.

7. MAINTAIN AND NOURISH HEALTHY RELATIONSHIPS

NO ONE WANTS TO HAVE UNHEALTHY RELATIONSHIPS, BUT SOMETIMES they just happen. Rather than dwell on the how and why of unhealthy relationships, your focus needs to be on how to maintain and nourish healthy relationships. This is key to overcoming depression and enjoying your life.

The drivers of healthy relationships can also protect you from depression and many other conditions. These drivers are feeling good about yourself (self-esteem) and doing good (positive engagement).

Feeling good about yourself (self-esteem)
The first relationship you need to feel good about is the one you have with yourself. This means that you value yourself for who you are and that you are able to have realistic expectations for yourself. The former means that you do not waste your time in useless comparisons with others and the latter means that you will have a reasonable expectation of meeting the goals you set for yourself.

Self-esteem grows from your beliefs and the thoughts that are generated based on those beliefs. You can neither buy it, borrow it, nor achieve it through cosmetic surgery. When your self-esteem is justified, you enjoy mental wellness and are taking an important step toward reducing the likelihood that you will become depressed.

Self-esteem is also intertwined with the capacity to face the stress of difficult situations and get back to a healthier place. This capacity is called resilience. The combination of self-esteem and resilience makes it possible to get through difficult times. People raised in a nurturing, supportive environment are more likely to have healthy self-esteem and resilience.

> Linda did not know for sure when her life changed, but she knew that "it" was still going on when she was 12 years old. She guessed that "it" had started earlier. It took years before she even acknowledged to herself what had happened. Linda was ashamed of her body and her behavior. She blamed herself for what had happened in her childhood. Linda thought that because she was successful she could put it all behind her without seeking professional help. As her life progressed, she began to realize that being sexually abused had affected her relationships with men and women, caused her anxiety, and resulted in her lifelong feelings of low self-esteem.

People who are raised in an environment that stifles their self-esteem are likely to end up as either having low self-esteem or going to the other extreme and having an over-inflated sense of their capacity to do anything. Both of these situations are unhealthy. People with an inflated sense of self end up destroying relationships because they consider themselves to be at the center of the universe. Those with low self-esteem have trouble forming healthy relationships and will often engage in destructive behaviors that alienate the very person they are trying to get closer to. Sometimes people with low self-esteem end up socially isolated and, as a result, get sick more often and die sooner than people who are socially connected.

With unhealthy levels of self-esteem, people may be impulsive and extremely overreactive to stress. They are also likely to end up either being abused or as the abuser because neither has healthy self-esteem. Additionally, people who are abusers tend to be manipulative. Like a vampire seeking a new victim, abusers know how to put on a good front so they attract the next person that they have selected as their prey. This occurs whether the abuser is a man or woman.

Self-esteem makes it possible for you to develop healthy boundaries between yourself and others. When you have healthy self-esteem, you know how and when to set limits on the invasiveness of others and in your interactions with others. This means that sometimes you have to say no. We often take on more responsibility than we should because we do not want to disappoint others. As a result, those values of work, endurance, and family need to be reined in once again. Healthy self-esteem means that sometimes you say yes but sometimes you also have to say no.

One of the important corollaries of this is that people with healthy self-esteem are as likely to say that they have a problem as they are to recognize that a problem is not theirs, but someone else's. Problem ownership is your awareness of whether a problem is your responsibility or someone else's and is key to establishing the healthy limits that are part of healthy self-esteem. This setting of healthy boundaries is fortified by being able to accurately assess where the problem actually lies. It is not about saying, "That is not my problem," but rather affirming that sometimes a situation is not within your scope of responsibility and control.

Feeling good about yourself allows you to build relationships based on common values and not because you are trying to compensate for feelings of inadequacy.

> Ignacio never knew that his son, Isaac, was so depressed that he had started using drugs. Isaac was doing well in school, he was involved in all sorts of sports, and he had lots of friends. How was anyone to know? Ignacio wept as he said, "He seemed like a normal kid."

Perhaps one of the areas that we overlook is the effect of poor self-esteem on children. Bad things happen to children. And when they occur, the results can last a long time. Children who suffer a major loss or trauma are at a greater risk of depression.

> Ernesto had been a patient of mine for many years. Every now and then he would come to see me because his depression would start to creep back and he would begin to get very anxious. One day when we were in session he had a major insight about what he had to do. He then looked at me and said, "I know that if I don't get up and do something, nothing will happen."

Doing good (positive engagement)

Healthy connections are key to avoiding or diminishing the effects of depression. In a healthy relationship, giving and receiving are done in a way that makes everyone feel that they are taken care of, valued, and respected. It is not just about giving, because that can leave us feeling drained, and it is not just about receiving, because that may leave the one doing the giving feeling abused or taken advantage of. Giving and receiving are complex actions.

In a study of primates by researchers at Roehampton University in London and the German Primate Center in Göttingen, Germany, the focus was on the effect of grooming behavior on levels of cortisol (the hormone that is produced in the presence of stress). The researchers knew that, for primates, the benefits of grooming were many—improved physical health, greater relaxation, and stronger social relationships.

What they did was to measure the levels of cortisol in animals that were being groomed and those that were the groomers. Although they could not account for their findings, they found that the groomers seemed to have less stress than the primates being groomed. In addition, the animals that spent the most time as groomers had the lowest levels of cortisol. While the investigators were able to document another benefit to grooming, they were left trying to figure out why the animal doing the grooming was less stressed than the one being groomed. If we apply this to what we know about people, then the results are not so unusual.

This finding is consistent with other findings that say that the happiest people are those who do work that they find rewarding. Perhaps the conclusion is simply that when we do what we enjoy, we are less stressed, and less stress translates into less depression. Likewise, the many benefits of altruism have been well-documented. Several studies have shown that people who volunteer are psychologically happier and their physical health is better than those who do not volunteer.

Your ability to feel good about who you are and your ability to do good are the first steps toward cultivating healthy relationships. One recurring theme in research findings is that good relationships are essential to our physical and mental health. There are many benefits to an active social network; while these networks are more common for women, they also have benefits for men.

The importance of healthy relationships was further highlighted in the Healthy Women Study. When marital satisfaction was high, marriage increased the likelihood of good health outcomes. Women who rated their relationships high on satisfaction had lower levels of biological, lifestyle, and psychosocial risk factors. A marriage that was rated poor was a better predictor of cardiovascular death in women than men. Based on the data, it seems that women have more physiological responses to marital conflict or disagreement than men do.

In light of these findings, it is not surprising that women show inconsistent health benefits from marriage while men consistently do better. These data may shift somewhat as the rate of same-sex marriage increases and is documented in the research.

Unfortunately, what experience demonstrates is that unhealthy relationships tend to be more demanding and less rewarding than healthy ones. We mistakenly believe that by focusing our time and energy on these unhealthy relationships we are taking care of people who rely on us. In reality, however, those relationships, which are rooted in someone's damaged self-esteem, are exhausting. The demands from the individual may change, but they will always be an emotional drain.

The challenge is to do the obvious, which is to nurture our healthy relationships because they are less demanding and much more rewarding.

8. KEEP A HEALTH JOURNAL

SINCE DEPRESSION CAN IMPAIR YOUR MEMORY OR EVEN YOUR ABILITY TO express yourself, finding an easy way to keep track of your health, including your mood, is important. When you visit your health care provider, your health journal can be an important source of information.

Writing is more than just keeping good records. Research shows that writing down what you are worried about actually helps people to do better. People who recorded their worries or emotions were found to do better on tests than people who were just given time to sit quietly.

9. CHERISH YOUR SPIRITUAL LIFE

THERE IS INCREASING EVIDENCE THAT RELIGIOUS INVOLVEMENT HAS A positive impact on a person's life. While many of us understand that faith is important to us, there is sometimes considerable social pressure to devalue the impact of faith with respect to our mental health. Initially, researchers claimed that people felt better because actively practicing their religion encouraged and bolstered social ties. Deeper analysis of the information showed that, regardless of which factors you took into account, participation in religious activities had a positive effect on depression for both men and women. Moreover, for women this finding was stronger than it was for men. Additionally, in further research it seemed that, for reasons that could not be teased out, religious involvement helped to reduce the stress that was experienced by more recent immigrants to the United States.

Taking part in religious activities is particularly helpful when those practices revolve around love and forgiveness. When the themes focus on punishment and guilt, the impact may be negative.

10. LISTEN TO YOUR BODY

WHEN IT COMES TO OVERCOMING DEPRESSION, ONE OF THE MOST important sources of information is your body. If you listen to your body, it will be easier to know when you are slipping into the depression zone.

Moving forward

How you experience depression varies depending on your personal history, triggering events, and the resources you have at hand. How you respond when you or someone you know is depressed can make all the difference between getting better or sinking more deeply into depression.

You start the 10-Point program by celebrating all the True answers to the self-assessment on page 60 because they are the positive actions you are already taking in your life. Then look at your False responses not as failures but as guideposts that tell you the direction in which you need to go.

To overcome your depression, it is important to think about what you have to do and not let your mind wander to unpleasant or negative thoughts. You need to stay focused in order to get to a better place. In the past, researchers believed that when people became sad that it made their mind wander. Recent research has documented that what happens is actually the reverse—when your mind wanders, it makes you unhappy.

So to manage your life in a way that will decrease the chances that you will become depressed again you need to focus on your selections from the 10-Point Program. This is not about making lists of things that you have to do that will never get done, but, rather, a way to acknowledge that to overcome depression and enjoy life you have to address the various elements that make up your life.

When you feel yourself getting pulled in the wrong direction—and you will have those moments—you need to pause and think about what you are doing. It is natural to slip up every now and then, but to avoid depression you need to regain your focus and get back on the program.

For Hispanics, responding in a way that is helpful means that you have to discard some common ideas about what depression is, who has depression, and how to manage it. To move forward you need to know and accept that depression is a real disorder, there is treatment for it, and there are actions that you can take to manage your life to reduce the likelihood of depression. The key things for you to remember are simple, as they are the basics for healthy living for you and your family. The 10-Point Program for Health and Wellness encourages and supports your efforts to overcome depression and have a healthier life.

Part Two

JUST
THE
FACTS

PART TWO PROVIDES THE MOST CURRENT INFORMATION ON THE TREAT-
ments that are available and other topics that are of interest to
anyone who is concerned about depression. Just as there is no
simple diagnostic test for depression, there is no treatment that
will work well in every instance. The treatments that are listed
here are the ones that you are most likely to encounter. Likewise,
the topics that are included reflect important areas where key
facts need to be made clear.

∿ Treatment

To be included in this section, the treatment had to have undergone clinical trials. Clinical trials compare the results from people who receive the treatment being studied to those that do not receive the treatment to determine whether a treatment is effective in treating a condition. There is great variability in the effectiveness of these treatments and in some instances there is even controversy, which is so noted. No treatment should be considered if it has not gone through a clinical trial. Each of the treatments described in the following section include information on what clinical trial data tell us about the treatment. More detailed information on how clinical trials are conducted can be found on page 99.

Cognitive behavior therapy (CBT)

Q Que pasa?
In this type of therapy, patients learn to take the facts they have and think about them in new ways (cognitive restructuring) and apply this new way of thinking to what they do (behavior). Both the therapist and the patient are actively engaged in this process. The therapist helps the patient sort through the facts, identify when his or her thoughts do not match the facts, and how his or her behavior needs to be consistent with what he or she now knows. In some cases CBT

COMPLEMENTARY AND ALTERNATIVE MEDICINE

encourages the patient to identify what is triggering the depression and to make necessary changes.

This type of therapy works to help you sort through your thoughts so that you can do the things you want to do. It also helps you to analyze and stop having thoughts and beliefs that produce maladaptive and unhealthy behaviors.

Q *Is it useful?*
CBT is very effective for people with minor to moderate depression. Some people may need CBT together with medication. CBT has also been documented to be effective in treating trauma-related disorders in children and teens.

Q *Any problems?*
For CBT to work, you must be able to talk honestly about what is going on in your life and be willing to make changes.

Complementary and alternative medicine (CAM)

Q *Que pasa?*
Officials at the National Center for Complementary and Alternative Medicine, part of the National Institutes of Health, readily admit that describing what is included under the umbrella of CAM is very difficult. According to these officials, CAM encompasses a group of diverse medical and health care systems, practices, and products that are not generally considered part of conventional

(Western or allopathic) medicine practiced by holders of MD (medical doctor) and DO (doctor of osteopathy) degrees and by allied health professionals, such as physical therapists, psychologists, and registered nurses. Different medical approaches include CAM to varying degrees, as for example:

- Complementary medicine: CAM together with conventional medicine.
- Alternative medicine: CAM in place of conventional medicine.
- Integrative medicine (also known as integrated medicine): Combines conventional and CAM treatments for which there is evidence of safety and effectiveness.

Very often, CAM includes use of a variety of herbal medicines (also known as botanicals), vitamins, minerals, and other "natural products." Many are sold over the counter as dietary supplements. Taking a multivitamin to meet minimum daily nutritional requirements or taking calcium to promote bone health are not thought of as CAM.

Is it useful?

Unknown. Results from clinical trials worldwide have been contradictory, and the effectiveness of St. John's wort, the most widely studied alternative treatment for depression, is still questionable.

Any problems?

The popular media often tout these alternative treatments, even in cases where evidence-based medicine has not proven their effectiveness. A greater concern is that a person's limited health care dollars will be wasted on products that do not deliver what they promise.

Interpersonal therapy (IPT)

Que pasa?

This treatment is considered short term because it is for 16 one-hour sessions that focus on one or two problems. It is a highly structured, manual-based intervention with three phases: a beginning (1–3 sessions), middle, and end (3 sessions). Once a person is diagnosed with depression, the problem is related to one of four areas: grieving, impasse in a relationship, getting through a major life transition (divorce or retirement), or having negative interpersonal behaviors. Sessions with a mental health professional involve talking about what is going on in your current life and developing skills and strategies to improve your life situation. For example, if your relationship is at an impasse, the work involves first deciding whether or not to end it. Once that decision is made, the focus in subsequent sessions is on what to do to move the relationship in the direction in which you want it to go. If the depression is in response to the death of a loved one, the initial sessions focus on allowing the person to grieve while later sessions address how to introduce new activities and relationships into the mourner's life to ease the loss.

This treatment is based on the belief that how someone interacts with others is a major factor in depression. The therapy works to improve communication and the way people relate to each other. It is viewed as less focused on thoughts and more in interpersonal dynamics.

Sometimes the therapist will work to identify painful trigger events from the past and guide the patient in ways to express the lingering emotions from those events in the present in a healthy way. Poor relationships from the past are analyzed by identifying the distorted thinking that led to problems, so a person can gain a more objective view of current relationships.

Q *Is it useful?*
IPT, which is usually used to treat depression and dysthymia, has varying degrees of effectiveness.

Q *Any problems?*
Some professionals view IPT as too limited in its duration and its focus. According to the International Society for Interpersonal Psychotherapy, IPT "addresses interpersonal issues in depression to the exclusion of all other foci of clinical attention."

Light therapy

Q *Que pasa?*
In this therapy a person is exposed to a light box that emits artificial light for a specific span of time in the morning, usually when it is still quite dark outdoors. Since the light produced is at the full spectrum, exposure to it is believed to reset the person's body rhythms.

You have to sit by the light box while you read, write, or eat. You do not look directly at the light. The length of time you have to sit is a function of the amount of light coming from the light box. A 10,000-lux illumination may require only 30 minutes of exposure while a 2,500-lux may require 2 hours. The technology is improving and there are cool-white, triphosphor, and biaxial lamps. These boxes are available for purchase at local pharmacies.

Q *Is it useful?*
This has been documented to be an effective treatment for people with seasonal affective disorder (SAD).

Q *Any problems?*
The amount and timing of exposure has to be determined for each person. There is increased interest in investigating the effectiveness of this therapy with other conditions.

Medication

Henry had no idea how the medication would help him. His entire life he had felt as if he were drowning in feelings of depression. He had managed to be successful because people only saw him for short periods. At the suggestion of his internist, Henry decided to try some medication. He reluctantly started to take his medication and after a few weeks could feel that something was different. The medication did not make him feel happy. What he felt was very unusual. For the first time, rather than going deeper into his depression, he felt as if something were lifting his chin and holding it up. These pills did not make him happy, but they did give him added support so that he did not feel as if he were drowning. He could look up and see that there was an alternative to being inundated in his own despair.

Q *Que pasa?*

Medications for depression are formulated to alter the chemistry in the brain. Depression may be treated with older medications, like tricyclics and monoamine oxidase inhibitors (MAOIs), or newer medicines, like selective serotonin reuptake inhibitors (SSRIs) or serotonin and norepinephrine reuptake inhibitors (SNRIs). There is no test to determine which medication will work best for a particular person and produce the fewest side effects. We know that MAOIs are effective in some people, but while taking them you need to be very attentive to foods and other medications to avoid serious complications. Most of the time, the medicines prescribed today are SSRIs or SNRIs because they are have fewer side effects. The generic forms of some of these are listed below in alphabetical order with the brand name in parentheses.

SSRIs

citalopram (Celexa)

escitalopram (Lexapro)

fluoxetine (Prozac)

fluvoxamine (Luvox)

paroxetine (Paxil)

sertraline (Zoloft)

SNRIs

desvenlafaxine (Pristiq)

duloxetine (Cymbalta)

venlafaxine (Effexor)

When you start taking psychotropic medication (that is, medicine designed to have an effect on the mind and address conditions like depression), if you want to stop taking it you need to discuss this with your health care provider.

There is strong evidence that smoking has an impact on how your body is able to use the medicines you take. Differences in how people respond to a medication can also be a function of age, how fast their body uses a drug, and how consistently they take their medication.

Q Is it useful?
According to NIMH, medication is most useful for someone who has moderate to severe depression, as determined by a health care provider. While there is no such thing as a "happy pill," you can overcome your depression if you take the medication that is best for you. To get the greatest benefit from your medication you should also be involved in psychotherapy.

It usually takes three to four weeks of consistently using a medication to know whether or not it works for you. If one medicine does not work, then your health care provider may recommend a different one. Usually, when people change medicines, they are able to find one that will work for them.

Q Any problems?
When it comes to children, experts contend that the medications available today are far from satisfactory. Furthermore, there are few new medicines in development and not enough research being conducted on the effectiveness of current medications for either children or adolescents.

Researchers do agree, however, that newer medicines have fewer side effects.

The biggest problem is that some people do not take their medicines as consistently as they should. Research confirms that people who are happier in their marriage are more likely to take their medication as required.

Psychoanalytic therapy

Que pasa?
This may be the most well-known type of therapy, but it is the least used today as a treatment for mental illness or mental health problems. This type of treatment, also known as psychoanalysis, is based on the work of Sigmund Freud. The sessions involve talking about how the unconscious mind influences what people are experiencing today. Considerable time and effort are also spent to uncover how childhood experiences contribute to current problems. As part of the treatment, the therapist may use techniques such as free association, dream interpretation, and role-playing. Treatment typically requires at least once-weekly sessions for several years.

Is it useful?
Comparative studies have documented that psychoanalysis is no more effective than a placebo.

Any problems?
The cost of psychoanalysis over a very long time and the intensive form of treatment involved in this approach may make it less appealing to most people.

Psychodynamic therapy

Q *Que pasa?*
Although this therapy was originally based in the theories of Sigmund Freud, over the years it has changed its focus to helping people gain greater self-awareness and understanding of their own actions. Some psychodynamic therapists use a combination, or eclectic, approach to treatment that includes other more behaviorally oriented therapy. It is both shorter in duration and less intense than psychoanalytic therapy and requires active involvement by the therapist.

Q *Is it useful?*
It all depends on the skill of your therapist.

Q *Any problems?*
According to the National Institute for Mental Health (NIMH), research into the effectiveness of this type of therapy has produced mixed results.

Psychotherapy

Elvira had suffered from depression for most of her life, but had learned to handle it. She did not care that she was not known as a cheery or positive person. Even as a child, she rarely smiled and often looked glum. Even though she felt this way, Elvira would usually do what she had to do regardless of feeling overwhelmed. She thought that this was the way life was supposed to be.

Q *Que pasa?*
Psychotherapy is the term given to all the treatments for mental health conditions that involve talking to a therapist. In this treatment, people are encouraged to talk about their feelings and their life situation to gain an understanding of their condition. In most instances, the first few sessions are spent obtaining information about the patient's life and the concerns she or he has. Based on their discussions, the therapist develops a treatment plan to meet the patient's needs. Depending on the diagnosis, medication may also be part of the treatment plan.

At the core of psychotherapy is the relationship between the patient and the therapist. This is a major factor in how effective the treatment will be.

When I was first training to be a clinical psychologist, I looked at my professor and commented that when I watched him it looked like he was just talking. He smiled, thanked me, and added that when you are really good at psychotherapy it looks like you are just talking. In the decades that I have seen patients, I have grown to appreciate that wisdom.

Psychotherapy is hard work for both the mental health professional and the person in therapy. The mental health professional needs to listen, process, and respond instantly to what is being said. The individual has to be honest and discuss what may be difficult or painful matters, listen, and use what he or she discusses to take the necessary steps in his or her life. Psychotherapy is not about having a one-hour session and feeling good afterwards. It is about the work you do when you are not in the session.

Q *Is it useful?*
Yes. There are different types of psychotherapy that are effective for specific problems. Both cognitive behavior therapy (see page 85) and IPT (see page 88) have worked well with people who are diagnosed with depression. I believe that for psychotherapy to be effective you need to see a licensed mental health professional who understands your language, celebrates your culture, and with whom you feel comfortable. The interpersonal dynamics are crucial because of the importance of building trust and respect. Part Three provides guidance on how to pick a therapist.

Q *Any problems?*
There are many types of therapies with new ones being developed on a regular basis. Sometimes the popularity of a particular therapy overshadows its effectiveness.

Stimulation Therapy (Brain stimulation therapy)

Q *Que pasa?*
These are very serious and controversial procedures that are reserved only for people with severe major depression that is very disabling and for whom no other treatments have worked. There are several types of therapies that fall in this category: electroconvulsive therapy (also known as ECT, or shock therapy), vagus nerve stimulation, repetitive transcranial magnetic stimulation, magnetic seizure therapy, and deep brain stimulation. In these treatments the brain is

stimulated by activating or touching the brain with magnets, implants, or an electrical current, as outlined below.

Electroconvulsive therapy (ECT)
A person is sedated with general anesthesia, and electrodes are placed at precise locations on one side of the head. Several short bursts of electricity are directed to the electrodes to induce a brain seizure. Patients undergoing ECT do not move because they are sedated. In most cases people undergo this treatment three times a week for up to 12 sessions to lift their depression. In this procedure the electrical current causes changes in the brain chemistry that are believed to stabilize the depression.

Vagus nerve stimulation (VNS)
The vagus nerve carries signals and messages from the part of your brain that controls mood, sleep, and other functions to your heart, lungs, liver, and stomach. In VNS, a person undergoes surgery to have a device similar to a pacemaker implanted under the skin in the upper left side of the chest. A wire is guided under the skin from the device to the vagus nerve. The device is programmed to send electrical impulses through the left vagus nerve on a set schedule. Although this was developed as a treatment for epilepsy in 2005, the FDA approved its use for major depression under very specific conditions.

Repetitive transcranial magnetic stimulation (rTMS)
In this procedure, a magnet is used to activate a specific site in the brain. An electromagnetic coil is placed on the forehead near the target area to deliver short electromagnetic pulses. The treatment lasts 30 to 60 minutes and does not require anesthesia.

Magnetic seizure therapy (MST)
This procedure, which requires general anesthesia, uses a very strong magnetic pulse at a specific area and induces a seizure.

Deep brain stimulation (DBS)
In DBS, electrodes implanted in your brain are connected to lead wires that connect to devices that are implanted on your chest. This procedure involves brain surgery and has all the associated risks. It was initially developed as a means to control the tremors and uncontrollable movements that characterize those with Parkinson's disease.

Q *Are these therapies useful?*
There is much research that needs to be done to understand the benefits and long-term risks of all these procedures.

Q *Any problems?*
Given the invasiveness of some of these procedures, the problems patients encounter are the ones that arise from general anesthesia, major surgery, and implants. Moreover, most of these have considerable side effects, and there is much research that needs to be done to determine how they work. For example, with rTMS the exact location of where to direct the electromagnetic stimulation is still under discussion. And while there has been much progress in the delivery of ECT since 1938, when it was first introduced, there is still controversy about how it works and its effect on memory.

∿ Other Topics

Clinical trials

Q *Que pasa?*
A clinical trial is a biomedical or health-related research study that has predefined who will be in a research study, the types of treatments that will be offered, and all the details of what will happen during and after the study.

Each study is designed to answer specific questions and that is why researchers carefully describe the characteristics you have to meet to be in the study (inclusion criteria) and those that exclude you from participation (exclusion criteria). Examples of the types of criteria are age, gender, the type and severity of a disease, previous treatment history, and other medical conditions.

Q *Are they useful?*
At this time clinical trials are the only way to know the effectiveness of a treatment.

Q *Any problems?*
One of the key concerns is obtaining *informed consent* from all participants in a clinical trial. Before agreeing to be a participant, you need to understand all aspects of what you have agreed to do. You and all other prospective participants must receive a written document that includes details about the purpose of the study, how long the study will last,

required procedures, risks and potential benefits, and key contacts. The document should be in the language you understand. After you have read the document and have had any questions answered, you can then decide whether or not to sign the document. Keep in mind that the informed consent document is not a contract; you can withdraw from a clinical trial at any time.

Mental health professionals

Q *Que pasa?*
There are many different kinds of mental health professionals. Here are some of the major ones with a short description of their training and what they can do. The type of psychotherapy that mental health professionals provide is based on the approach they choose to follow. The list below is in alphabetical order.

Licensed professional counselors earn a master's degree (MA) in psychology, counseling, or a similar discipline and typically have at least two years of postgraduate experience. They may provide services that include diagnosis and counseling (individual, family/group, or both).

Psychiatric/mental health nurses may have degrees ranging from associate to doctoral level (DNSc, PhD). Depending on their education and licensing, they provide a broad range of services, including assessment, case management, and psychotherapy. In certain states, some psychiatric nurses may prescribe and monitor medication.

Psychiatrists are physicians who earned an MD or OD degree and have at least four more years of specialized study and training in psychiatry. Psychiatrists are licensed as physicians to practice medicine by individual states. "Board-certified" psychiatrists have passed the national examination administered by the American Board of Psychiatry and Neurology. Psychiatrists provide medical and psychiatric evaluations, offer psychotherapy, and prescribe and monitor medications.

Psychologists include people who have a master's degree (MA or MS) in psychology; a doctoral degree (PhD) in clinical, counseling, or research psychology; a doctorate in psychology that focuses on applied work (PsyD); or a doctorate in education (EdD). Most states have licensing requirements for people to practice psychology; these require psychologists to pass national and state exams. A psychologist is licensed to administer psychological tests, conduct evaluations, and provide psychotherapy. In New Mexico, some licensed psychologists may prescribe and monitor medication.

Psychopharmacologists are usually psychiatrists who specialize in the use of psychiatric drugs to manage mental disorders.

Social workers may have a bachelor's degree, a master's degree (MSW), or a doctoral degree (DSW or PhD). Most states license social workers after they pass an examination to be licensed to practice social work (LCSW). Social workers provide various services, including case management, hospital discharge planning, and psychotherapy.

Q *Any problems?*
The differences among these professionals are sometimes very subtle, but they may be important to you. For example, a psychologist who holds a PsyD degree is trained to be a practicing psychologist (sees patients) and someone who uses research findings, while a psychologist with a PhD in clinical psychology has more years of training and is trained to be both a practicing psychologist and a researcher.

Positive psychology

Q *Que pasa?*
This relatively new area of psychology has received much attention. The term was coined in 1998 by Dr. Martin E. P. Seligman and Dr. Mihaly Csikszentmihalyi because the focus of their work was on well-being and happiness.

Q *Is it useful?*
Most definitely. In positive psychology, mental health is not just the absence of mental illness but also the presence of positive emotions and traits. In 2004, Dr. Christopher Peterson and Dr. Seligman took a major step in creating a classification system for the character strengths and virtues (CSVs) that are most essential to develop for our total mental wellness. In their book, *Character Strengths and Virtues: A Handbook and Classification,* they identified six major virtues that we need to have in order to enjoy well-being and happiness.

VIRTUES AND CHARACTER STRENGTHS

Wisdom and knowledge: creativity, curiosity (interest, novelty-seeking, openness to experience), open-mindedness (judgment, critical thinking), love of learning, and perspective (wisdom)

Courage: bravery, persistence (perseverance, industrious-ness), integrity (authenticity, honesty), and vitality (zest, enthusiasm, vigor, and energy)

Humanity: love, kindness (generosity, nurturance, care, compassion, altruistic love, "niceness"), and social intelligence (emotional intelligence, personal intelligence)

Justice: citizenship (social responsibility, loyalty, team-work), fairness, and leadership

Temperance: forgiveness and mercy, humility and modesty, prudence, and self-regulation (self-control)

Transcendence: appreciation of beauty and excellence (awe, wonder, elevation), gratitude, hope (optimism, future-mindedness, future orientation), humor (play-fulness), and spirituality (religiousness, faith, purpose)

Source: Christopher Peterson and Martin E. P. Seligman, Character Strengths and Virtues: A Handbook and Classification *(Oxford, UK: Oxford University Press, 2004).*

Results from other studies also confirm the importance of positive relationships. Many studies have documented that when the quality of the relationship between parents is high, their children have better outcomes. The data indicate that happy parental relationships are consistently related to better outcomes for children across all economic, racial, ethnic, and family-structure lines.

Q *Any problems?*
The major issue involving positive psychology is the popular misconception about what it is. It is about more than smiling. Data drawn from studies of positive psychology show that life satisfaction and positive emotions strongly contribute to and correlate with better overall health and a longer life.

Stress

Q *Que pasa?*
When stress is unresolved it wears us down and can lead to depression. That is why it is essential that we know what causes unhealthy stress in our lives and what we can do to reduce it.

How we handle stress ranges somewhere along the dimension of "fight or flight" or "tend and befriend." For many years fight or flight was the only explanation for how people handled stress. Specifically, when you received stress signals, your body would prepare you to either fight or get out of the situation. Most of these data were based on studies of men.

More recent research has documented that women facing stress generally use a strategy of "tend and befriend," rather than "fight or flight." According to these findings, when women are under stress they rely on their social networks for support. But rather than men and women having two different strategies in response to stress, more likely each individual's response to stressful events is also determined by the situation. If someone is about to attack a woman, then "tend and befriend" certainly would not be in her best interest. Regardless of which strategy someone decides to follow, the reality is that when you have more stress, your body will continue to produce more cortisol. And that is not good because more cortisol makes it hard for your immune cells to function properly.

Keep in mind that "tend and befriend" has been hypothesized as perhaps one of the reasons women live longer than men. The data indicate that among the ways men generally respond to stress are aggression, social withdrawal, and substance abuse. Recent research documents that it is the individual's perception of loneliness, regardless of whether or not they are alone, that leads to stress and depression.

Q Is it useful?

All of us have some stress in our lives and up to a point stress is good. It serves as a motivator and helps us keep our senses sharp. But excess stress or stress that is unresolved can lead to depression. Most people state that the major stressors in their lives have to do with work and money. When Hispanics were asked the same question, they identified family health as their major source of stress.

Q Any problems?

The major problem here is that some people believe that you should simply cope with stress. Actually you need to eliminate excess stress from your life. Researchers in social genomics have confirmed that chronic adversity, such as stress, affects your immune system at the molecular level.

Suicide

This time Teresa felt different. She seemed to be sinking deeper into her negative feelings. Orlando, her husband, and all of her children knew that Mommy was not okay. Every attempt they made to help her seemed instead to push her deeper into the abyss of sadness that seemed to be engulfing her.

Teresa looked at her house and saw how it was increasingly messy and her papers were all over the kitchen counters. And although she wanted to, Teresa was unable to get out of her bed in the morning, even when she knew she had to take her children to school before she went to work at the job she had never particularly liked. Orlando did not know what to do and became petrified when Teresa said, "I feel like driving the car into a wall."

Q *Que pasa?*
Suicide is a major problem in the United States for all of us. It remains the eighth leading cause of death for people of all ages. It is a problem for young people but an even greater problem among those over 65. Specifically, in 2004 there were 4,599 suicides among Americans ages 10 to 24, up from 4,232 in 2003, for a rate of 7.32 per 100,000 people that age. While that rate is high, it was nearly twice as high for people over 65 (14.3 of every 100,000 people).

Mental health providers have been increasingly concerned about the potential for suicide among people under their

SUICIDE

care, regardless of their diagnosis. The prevention of suicide has become so critical that beginning with DSM-V, clinicians will be asked to rate the potential for suicide of all patients under their care from lowest concern to imminent concern. In rating the potential for suicide, the clinician will take into account long-term factors (history of suicide attempt by the individual or a close family member or friend, mental illness, abuse, chronic pain, anger, and aggressiveness), stressful events within the last three months (loss, psychiatric discharge or admission, increase in alcohol abuse, worsening of symptoms of depression), and stressful events within the last week (feelings of hopelessness, marked anxiety, plans for suicide, or person is living alone). The rating will be used to determine the importance of suicide prevention as part of developing a treatment plan for the person. It is not meant to be used as a tool to predict whether or not someone will attempt suicide.

There are many risk factors for suicide. These include depression, various mental disorders, substance abuse disorder, or some combination of these. These risk factors account for 90 percent of the cases where a person's death is due to suicide.

If you or someone you know is considering suicide, it is imperative to get professional help as soon as possible. You can call 911 or go to the nearest emergency room for help. Additionally, remove all firearms and other potential means to commit suicide.

Any problems?
Men outnumber women who commit suicide by a ration of 4.5:1. For every suicide, there are anywhere from 8 to 25 attempts.

Part Three

RESOURCES AND TOOLS

If you have questions about depression, please call the National Hispanic Family Health Help Line at 1-866-783-2645 or 1-866-SU-FAMILIA. Health promotion advisors are available to answer your questions in English and Spanish and to help you find local services. You can call Monday through Friday, from 9 A.M. to 6 P.M., Eastern time.

You can also contact the National Suicide Prevention Lifeline. This service sponsored by the U.S. Department of Health and Human Services is a free, 24-hour hotline available to anyone, or someone you care about, in suicidal crisis or emotional distress. By calling the line you will be routed to the nearest crisis center to you among 150 participating crisis centers nationwide. For services in English, call 1-800-273-TALK (8255). For services in Spanish, call 1-888-628-9454. On both lines, veterans or their families and friends can press 1 and they will be connected to a Veterans Administration professional and services tailored for veterans.

The National Alliance on Mental Illness operates an information helpline available by calling 1-800-950-NAMI (6264), Monday through Friday, 10 A.M. to 6 P.M., Eastern time.

BEST NONCOMMERCIAL WEBSITES

While there are many sites that offer to treat depression with a product or a process, the websites listed below are dedicated to providing you the best information available and will not sell any personal information you provide. Additionally, none of these sites allow for advertising or product endorsements.

MENTAL HEALTH AMERICA
www.nmha.org
(formerly known as the National Mental Health Association)
Mental Health America is a network of more than 300 local affiliates that provide access to a broad range of self-help and professional services; housing and supported employment; access to comprehensive mental health screenings; and individual follow-up to secure effective treatment.

NATIONAL ALLIANCE FOR HISPANIC HEALTH
www.hispanichealth.org
The Alliance is committed to improving the health and well-being of Hispanics and working with others to secure health for all.

NATIONAL INSTITUTE FOR MENTAL HEALTH (NIMH)
www.nimh.nih.gov
The mission of NIMH is to transform the understanding and treatment of mental illnesses through basic and clinical research, paving the way for prevention, recovery, and cure.

NATIONAL ALLIANCE ON MENTAL ILLNESS (NAMI)

www.nami.org

NAMI's efforts are focused on educating America about mental illness, offering resources to those in need, and advocacy efforts to ensure that mental illness is a high national priority.

NATIONAL INSTITUTE OF NEUROLOGICAL DISORDERS AND STROKE

www.ninds.nih.gov

The mission of NINDS is to reduce the burden of neurological disease —a burden borne by every age group, by every segment of society, by people all over the world.

NATIONAL LIBRARY OF MEDICINE (NLM): MEDLINE PLUS

www.nlm.nih.gov

The NLM is part of the National Institutes of Health and is the world's largest medical library. The Library collects materials and provides information and research services in all areas of biomedicine and health care.

THE CARTER CENTER MENTAL HEALTH PROGRAM

www.cartercenter.org/health/mental_health/

Under the leadership of former First Lady Rosalynn Carter, the nation's foremost champion for the rights of people with mental illnesses, the Carter Center's Mental Health Program works to promote awareness about mental health issues, reduce stigma and discrimination against those with mental illnesses, and achieve greater parity for mental health in the U.S. health care system.

QUESTIONS TO ASK YOUR HEALTH CARE PROVIDER

Questions about treatment for depression

- *How can you help me with my depression?*
- *Is there anything else that I should do?*
- *Is there medication that I can take?*
- *What are the side effects of this medication?*
- *How long will I have to take this medication?*
- *Are there any alternatives to taking medication?*
- *Should I see a psychotherapist?*
- *Do you have any recommendations?*

Questions about medications for depression

- *What is the name of the medication that you want me to take?*
- *How much will I be taking?*
- *When do I take it?*
- *Are there any special instructions about how to take it?*
- *How long will I have to take it?*
- *How long will it be before it starts to work?*
- *What happens if I forget to take a pill?*
- *Are there any side effects that I should be concerned about?*
- *How often will I see you about my medication?*
- *Are there any interactions with the other medicines, supplements, teas, and over-the-counter products I am taking?*

How to pick a psychotherapist

When you pick your psychotherapist, your choice will be based on affordability and how well the two of you communicate with each other. Here are some of the steps you need to take and some of the information you need to obtain.

1. Get names

• *Ask your health care provider for recommendations.*

• *Ask other people you know for their suggestions.*

2. Before making an appointment, call the office and obtain some basic information about the person and the practice

License. *Make sure you know the type of mental health professional you are consulting and that he or she is licensed. Licensing means a person met educational requirements from an institution that is accredited, met your state's standards for the profession, agreed to follow and be held to a code of ethical conduct, and earns continuing education credits on an ongoing basis. Although the licenses that are required vary by state, I strongly recommend that, when you are looking for a psychotherapist, he or she be licensed as a psychiatrist, a psychologist, or a social worker. It is troubling that in most states anyone can claim to be a therapist or counselor without having to earn a license.*

Language. *Make sure the therapist speaks your language. This does not mean that you can pick someone just because he or she has a familiar last name.*

Hours of operation. *The hours need to match your schedule, based on the flexibility you have during the day.*

THE BUENA SALUD GUIDE TO OVERCOMING DEPRESSION

Fees. *You need to know what it will cost for the first visit and for future sessions. In many practices, the fee for the first visit may be waived and the session may be shorter than the typical 45–50–minute session. It is also good to know about any of the following that may be important to you:*

• *What type of insurance is accepted? Medicare? Medicaid?*

• *Does he or she accept direct billing to or payment from your insurance company?*

• *Is there is a sliding-scale fee policy?*

• *Does he or she take credit cards?*

3. DURING YOUR FIRST VISIT, MAKE SURE TO GET INFORMATION ABOUT THE FOLLOWING:

Expertise. *Ask about the psychotherapist's areas of expertise.*

Experience. *You should ask about the therapist's experience with similar problems.*

Treatment. *Ask about treatments that have been successful for people with similar problems and how long people who were successfully treated had to stay in therapy.*

Value. *Through your interaction, your prospective therapist should make you feel that he or she values you and your culture.*

Most important, be aware of how well the therapist listens to what you have to say. In most types of psychotherapy, the relationship you have with your therapist will be key for your progress. Your ability to feel comfortable with him or her is essential. If you feel that you cannot talk about your feelings or experiences with him or her, then you should be seeing someone else.

TRACKING WHAT YOU DO

"What I Am Doing" gives you a way to keep track of your mood, how healthy you are eating, social interactions, medication(s), sleep, and exercise. If you regularly write down what you are doing in these areas, you will be able to provide your mental health care provider with timely and valuable information that can help in the fine-tuning of your treatment plan. You can also use this chart to see what factors change how your body feels and what is your overall mood from day to day. It is good to be able to identify what is helpful and what is damaging in your life.

To track your mood, how healthy you are eating, and how you feel about your social interactions use the scale below and for the other items fill in the information as indicated.

1 = *extremely negative*   5 = *slightly positive*
2 = *moderately negative*   6 = *moderately positive*
3 = *slightly negative*   7 = *extremely positive*
4 = *neutral*

Mood: *How did you feel most of the day?*

Food: *How would you describe your overall food choices?*

Social: *How do you feel about your interactions with others throughout the day?*

All Meds: *Did you take all of your medicines? The answer here is yes or no.*

Sleep: *How many <u>hours</u> did you sleep last night?*

Exercise: *How many <u>minutes</u> of exercises did you do?*

Notes: *Add any information that you feel is important about the day.*

WHAT I AM DOING

(Scale of 1 = extremely negative to 7 = extremely positive)

Date	Mood (1–7)	Food (1–7)	Social (1–7)	All Meds (Yes/No)	Sleep (Hours)	Exercise (Minutes)	Notes

ᴖAcknowledgments

There are many people who make the *Buena Salud*™ series possible. The entire team at Newmarket Press, especially Esther Margolis, Heidi Sachner, Keith Hollaman, and Harry Burton, has provided incredible encouragement. The board, staff, and members of the National Alliance for Hispanic Health and the Health Foundation for the Americas also nurtured the series.

Much of this book is also about my patients and their struggles and hard work. These individuals knew they had a problem and made the decision to work on getting better. I am humbled for all they have shared with me and all the steps that they continue to take to make their lives and the lives of those they love better.

I want to give many thanks to Mrs. Rosalynn Carter for her foreword and her decades of leadership. She inspires many by her generosity, kindness, and tenaciousness. The thoughtful comments provided by Dr. Alan I. Leshner, CEO, American Association for the Advancement of Science, helped to increase the impact of this book.

The personal support that I need to write comes from my life sisters and brothers as well as exceptional friends and include Kevin Adams, Carolyn Curiel, Msgr. Duffy, Adolph P. Falcón, Polly Gault, Paula Gomez, Ileana Herrell, Thomas Pheasant, Bob Presbie, Sheila Raviv, Carolina Reyes, Esther Sciammarella, Amanda Spivey, Cynthia A. Telles, and Elizabeth Valdez.

My relationship with Margaret Heckler spans nearly three decades, throughout which she has shared her extensive knowledge, belief in the greater good, her deep faith, and the importance of faith in everyone's life. My memories and experiences with my extraordinary mother Lucy Delgado, my cousin Deborah Helvarg, and my friend Henrietta Villaescusa are also part of part of everything that I am and all that I do. And most of all on a daily basis the love and support of my husband, Mark, and daughter, Elizabeth, have been essential to my life.

INDEX

INDEX

ABOUT THE AUTHOR

JANE L. DELGADO, Ph.D., M.S., author of *The Latina Guide to Health: Consejos and Caring Answers* and *The Buena Salud™ Guides*, is President and Chief Executive Officer of the National Alliance for Hispanic Health ("the Alliance"), the nation's largest organization of health and human service providers to Hispanics. She was recognized by the *Ladies' Home Journal* as one of the "Ladies We Love" in 2010 and by *WebMD* as one of its four Health Heroes of 2008 for her dedication and resilience in advocacy. Among many other awards and honors, in 2007 *People En Español* named her to the 100 Influentials in the Hemisphere.

A practicing clinical psychologist, Dr. Delgado joined the Alliance in 1985 after serving in the Immediate Office of the Secretary of the U.S. Department of Health and Human Services (DHHS), where she became a key force in the development of the landmark "Report of the Secretary's Task Force on Black and Minority Health."

At the Alliance, Dr. Delgado oversees the national staff as well as field operations throughout the United States, Puerto Rico, and the District of Columbia. She serves on the National Biodefense Science Board. She is also a trustee of the Kresge Foundation, Lovelace Respiratory Research Institute, and the Northern Virginia Health Foundation, and serves on the national advisory councils for the Paul G. Rogers Society for Global Health Research and on the National Board of Mrs. Rosalynn Carter's Task Force on Mental Health.

Dr. Delgado received her M.A. in Psychology from New York University in 1975. In 1981 she was awarded a Ph.D. in clinical psychology from SUNY Stony Brook and an M.S. in Urban and Policy Sciences from the W. Averell Harriman School of Urban and Policy Sciences. She lives in Washington, D.C., with her husband, Mark, and daughter, Elizabeth.

Founded in 1973, the **National Alliance for Hispanic Health** is the foremost science-based source of information and trusted advocate for the health of Hispanics. The Alliance represents local community agencies serving more than 15 million persons each year, and national organizations serving over 100 million persons, making a daily difference in the lives of Hispanic communities and families.

The **Health Foundation for the Americas (**HFA) supports the work and mission of the National Alliance for Hispanic Health. Every year HFA supports programs to improve health for all by helping secure clean air to breathe, clean water to drink, safe places to play, and healthy food to eat. HFA and the Alliance help those without healthcare gain access to free and low-cost services where they live and improve the quality of healthcare. The programs put new health technology to work in communities, provide millions of dollars in science and health career scholarships, and conduct the research and advocacy that is transforming health.

You can be a part of this extraordinary mission of health and well-being. To learn more about the Alliance or the HFA, visit www.hispanichealth.org or www.healthyamericas.org.

The author donates all royalties from the Spanish editions of her books to The Health Foundation for the Americas (HFA).

Newmarket Titles by Jane L. Delgado

Written specifically for the growing U.S. Hispanic population by Jane L. Delgado, Ph.D., M.S., the president and CEO of the National Alliance for Hispanic Health, *The Buena Salud™ Guides* present the best in science and health advice, available in both English and Spanish-language editions.

The Buena Salud™ Guide to Diabetes and Your Life
Introduction by Larry Hausner, CEO, America Diabetes Association

Featuring the stories of people and families living with diabetes—a condition that has touched the lives of most Hispanic families—this concise guide explains everything readers need to know, including the important fact that diabetes is not inevitable.

The book discusses: the factors that contribute to developing diabetes and how to prevent it; the types and evolving definition of diabetes; how the endocrine and immune systems function; the impact of the environment on diabetes; treatment options, including medication and realistic changes in lifestyle and diet; and features an A-Z section with all commonly used diabetes terms.

Paperback • 128 pages • ISBN: 978-1-55704-941-4 • $9.95

Also available in Spanish:
La guía de Buena Salud™ sobre la diabetes y tu vida (978-1-55704-942-1)

The Buena Salud™ Guide for a Healthy Heart
Introduction by Jack Lewin, M.D., CEO, American College of Cardiology

Opening with a personal story from Dr. Delgado about her mother's experience with heart disease, this invaluable guide details everything readers need to know about the leading cause of death for all men and women in the U.S.

The book explains: how the heart works; how heart problems develop and what can be done to avoid them; achievable lifestyle changes to maintain heart health; and features an A-Z section with all commonly used heart terms.

Paperback • 128 pages • ISBN: 978-1-55704-943-8 • $9.95

Also available in Spanish:
La guía de Buena Salud™ para un corazón sano (978-1-55704-944-5)

ALSO BY JANE L. DELGADO, PH.D., M.S.

The Buena Salud™ Guide to Overcoming Depression and Enjoying Life
Foreword by Former First Lady Rosalynn Carter
  Founder, Carter Center Mental Health Program

Highlighted by real-life stories, this authoritative, accessible guide answers the most asked questions about depression, debunks common myths, and offers readers information they can trust on treating and managing this condition.

The book addresses: how to overcome cultural barriers to recognizing and seeking help for depression, including *machismo* and *aguantando* (enduring); the relationship between depression and chronic conditions such as diabetes, heart disease, and arthritis; medication, therapy options, genetics, alternative treatments; lifestyle changes to help overcome depression; the social and physical differences in how men and women deal with depression; advice on choosing a psychotherapist; and an A-Z section covering commonly used depression terms.

Paperback • 128 pages • ISBN: 978-1-55704-972-8 • $9.95

Also available in Spanish:
La guía de Buena Salud™ para superar la depresión y disfrutar la vida (978-1-55704-974-2)

The Latina Guide to Health: Consejos and Caring Answers
Foreword by Antonia Novello, M.D., M.P.H., Dr. P.H., Former U.S.
  Surgeon General

Featuring cutting-edge medical information and advice fo all Hispanic women, Dr. Delgado offers practicial information on the health issues women face, separates myths from facts, and answers questions about what to do. She discusses arthritis, cervical cancer, depression, and other important topics in a quick-reference health section.

Paperback • 240 pages • ISBN: 978-1-55704-854-7 • $15.95

Also available in Spanish:
La guía de salud: Consejos y respuestas para la mujer latina (978-1-55704-855-4)

The Buena Salud™ Guide for a Healthy Heart
_____ copies at $9.95 each
La guía de Buena Salud™ para un corazón sano
_____ copies at $9.95 each

The Buena Salud™ Guide to Diabetes and Your Life
_____ copies at $9.95 each
La guía de Buena Salud™ sobre la diabetes y tu vida
_____ copies at $9.95 each

The Buena Salud™ Guide to Overcoming Depression and Enjoying Life
_____ copies at $9.95 each
La guía de Buena Salud™ para superar la depresión y disfrutar la vida
_____ copies at $9.95 each

The Latina Guide to Health: Consejos and Caring Answers
_____ copies at $15.95 each
La guía de salud: Consejos y respuestas para la mujer latina
_____ copies at $15.95 each

For postage and handling, add $5.00 for the first book, plus $1.50 for each additional book. Please allow 4–6 weeks for delivery. Prices and availability subject to change.

I enclose a check or money order, payable to Newmarket Press, in the amount of $_____. (New York State residents, please add applicable sales tax.)

Name _____

Address _____

City/State/Zip _____

Special discounts are available for orders of five or more copies.
For information, contact Newmarket Press, Special Sales Dept.,
18 East 48th Street, New York, NY 10017
Phone: (212) 832-3575 or (800) 669-3903; Fax: (212) 832-3629
E-mail: sales@newmarketpress.com • www.newmarketpress.com